My Story in Colour

by New Forest Artist
Suzan Houching

To Delyth
Best Wishes
Suzan Houching

Editing and layout by Jenny Knowles

First published in 2015
Publisher – Little Knoll Press

ISBN No. 978-0-9927220-5-0

Copies of this book can be obtained from
www.LittleKnollBookshop.co.uk
and from bookshops by request.

Printed in Great Britain by
Hobbs the Printers Ltd.
Totton, Hampshire

DEDICATION

I dedicate this book to my husband, Ted. He was a quiet, thoughtful, methodical man, and after nearly twenty years at sea, was content to live in a house crammed to the rafters with paintings, paints, brushes, books and fishing gear, plus an assortment of family and pets!

His support for my art, his constant supply of cups of tea and marmite toast as I worked, and his well considered opinions on what I was painting at the time, were invaluable.

He was pleased about my book and how it was bringing my paintings and stories together, and I just wish he had lived long enough to see it completed. He was, after all, the happy inspiration behind much of it.

Thank you Ted.

ACKNOWLEDGEMENTS

My grateful thanks go to all the people who helped make this book possible – to family and friends, The Woodlanders, and the owners of paintings; Major Mike Allan who has nineteen of them, Lord Bath who has six, and numerous families from Burley village and as far afield as Australia who have one or more on their walls. Thank you also to New Forest Cider, ExxonMobil and the National Motor Museum, Beaulieu, for allowing the inclusion of work I did for them.

Of the pubs that I've written about, The Stocks Inn and The Coventry Arms still have the same names, and I'm pleased that the present owners and management are happy to see them featuring in my stories.

I have spoken to most of the people whom I've mentioned in the book and thank them for their kind permission. There remain just a few people that I have not been able to contact and I hope that you will also be happy to be part of 'My Story'.

Thank you also to Jenny Knowles, who thought of the idea and spent so much time painstakingly laying out the pages, and to the kind man who helped her with the line editing (he will know who he is).

I feel very privileged to have such a lovely Foreword written by Hannah Gordon. I hope you, dear reader, will enjoy this book too.

The Flight of the Seagull

FOREWORD
by Hannah Gordon

It was a cold winter's afternoon and a parcel had arrived for me. Inside was a folder containing Suzan Houching's book, *My Story in Colour*. As I turned the pages I found myself being immediately drawn into a wonderful, sunny world.

Suzan's book is full of her glorious paintings, each telling a story, or stories, in pictures as well as in words. She seems to be one of those rare people, just as at home with a pen as with a paint brush. Her keen observation of life and the funny things that happen made me laugh. Not every character is necessarily attractive, but all of them are amusingly and kindly portrayed.

Suzan's generous spirit is obvious to anyone the minute they meet her, just as it was when I first encountered her at a Woodlanders Art Exhibition. Her book, with so many stories about her big and close-knit family, could make anyone with a small family quite envious, but it is wonderful that she has shared all her experiences with us. It is a book that you can sit down and read, or one that you can dip into.

I shall visit it often and with great pleasure.

Suzan, Ted (Suzan's husband) and Hannah Gordon
at The Woodlanders Art Exhibition preview

PICTURE INDEX

This is my idea of an ideal village, with a farm, a pub, a school, shops, a wedding and a church, but as usual it is a fictitious place.

PAINTING

I have always painted and drawn as far back as I can remember.

Our four eldest grandchildren, Robyn, Jordan, Georgi and Joe, are all creative, each in their own way, and now our youngest grandson, Ethan, is at the stage of wanting to make exciting marks on drawing paper, or wet sand when we go down to the beach.

At the turn of one year into another, on the stroke of midnight I always make a drawing in my sketchbook. Up to now it has been of my husband, Ted, watching the fireworks on television.

Art lessons at my first school, Southlands, were enjoyable, then a little more staid at my second school, Melverley School, in Wimborne. There, we only had one 40 minute lesson a week, which to most girls was a relief, but to me, a disappointment. Although I love patterns, the 'pattern' of our lessons was predictable; three weeks of still life, three weeks of pattern making, i.e. week 1 – design a motive, week 2 – trace and repeat your motive on a piece of paper, and week 3 – actually paint the thing, by which time we were heartily fed up with the whole idea. The third set of three weeks was my favourite – composition.

My love of Dylan Thomas's work exploded at one particular art lesson, when out of the blue, we were each given an extract from *Under Milk Wood* and told to illustrate it. Mine was of the postman, Willy Nilly, and his wife in their kitchen, steaming open letters before Willy Nilly went on his round to deliver them. I was absolutely hooked, and my love of painting ordinary people going about their own business or portraying villages and their various activities, stems from that afternoon.

My boat and harbour paintings are again from my imagination, and if I need reference, I use my sketch book work, sometimes completed many years ago.

If anyone asks me what I think is the most useful thing to help you as an artist, I say without fail, a sketch book and pen.

Keep them in your pocket at all times, you never know what might take your eye.

Cameras can be handy for quickness and reminders, but they are not quite the same. If you concentrate your mind on something and discover how it works by actually drawing it, then it stays in your mind. Photographs can evoke memories, but your own sketchbooks are part of YOU, and very personal.

RED and GREEN together

It must have been autumn, as David was still a young baby – we were sharing a double pram with two hoods, like an egg, and being pushed along our lane. David was at the far end and fast asleep.

I was fascinated by what I now know to be rowan trees. I loved the glossy green leaves and bright red berries. It started to rain and whoever was pushing us – it might have been our Aunt Rene – closed the hoods.

I remember screaming loudly with rage and fear, as we were virtually in the dark and I couldn't see 'my trees'.

The hoods were re-opened.

To this day I don't like closed doors or curtains. They are always open in my paintings, but like any self-respecting country girl, I always shut gates.

In the photo, I am sitting in the double-hooded pram, looking at my brother Paul, who appears to be having a Simon Cowell moment with his trousers.

My mother loved prams and it seems they were always changing.

I longed for a beautiful doll's pram, with large fine wheels and shiny bright paint, but what appeared one birthday when I was small, was a little, dumpy pram with small fat wheels, and I didn't like it. My brothers did, and, as in the case of my bicycle many years later, it made a good go-cart.

My parents must have gone to great lengths to even find a toy pram, as it was only a few years since the end of the war. Toys weren't a priority and I still feel sorry for my reaction.

RED and WHITE

I love to use red and white together, especially in patterns on fabric.

I have a vivid memory of the day my brother, David, and I were playing in the dairy yard with a little boy much younger than us. He was the small grandson of one of the men on the farm. I can't remember his name, but I do know he had lost his mother when he was little more than a baby.

He and his mother were blackberrying one day, he one side of the lane and she the other. She ran across the lane to stop the little boy from toddling into the path of an oncoming army lorry – with fatal results for herself.

His grandparents were bringing him up and he was a happy boy.

I'm not sure what we were playing, but David gave the little boy a piggy-back and reluctantly allowed himself to be given a piggy-back in return.

David was older and much heavier, so the inevitable happened and he fell, cutting his forehead badly on a rusty feeding bin, blood everywhere. I grabbed David's hand and we ran up to the farmhouse for help. At the time we were in our school uniforms and, as I looked at my brother's white shirt front splattered with drops of blood, my thoughts were, 'That looks wonderful!'

DARK GREEN

It was August 15th 1950, and we were living in Merley, near Wimborne, where years later *Top Gear* filmed their programme in which the campervan went up in flames.

Three things happened on that day in my memory.

First of all, it was the day Princess Anne was born, much to the delight of my father, who so respected the Royal Family that if the National Anthem was played, under any circumstances he would shoot to his feet.

Secondly, it was the day my father decided to paint the front gate dark green. David and I stood watching him with curiosity. It was raining and the paint seemed to be bubbling, but he made it clear that he could do without our unasked-for advice.

Thirdly, our real reason for being there was not to annoy our father, but because we had heard a conversation between our parents that morning. Apparently, the 'new man next door' had tried to drown his wife in the bath, and we wanted to see what a would-be murderer looked like. When he drove into their drive, looking just like anyone else, we lost interest and went indoors to see what Paul was doing. He was upstairs, reading as usual.

Father was glad to be left alone in the rain to finish painting.

KHAKI - Soldiers' Uniforms

I was the sort of child that liked to stand and watch people and all the daft things they got up to.

We were all told not to go into the front garden during the afternoon as our mother needed to rest, and we made too much noise. On this day, I crept round to the front porch away from my brothers and sat down.

Our house was on the road between the Army camp and the town, so it wasn't unusual to see soldiers walking past. I sat there hoping no one would notice me, when one of a group of soldiers passed by and threw a bag of sweets into the garden.

It was 1950 and sweet rationing was still on, but having been warned in no uncertain manner about taking sweets from strangers, for once I did the right thing and took them straight upstairs to my mother.

She was still in bed resting, but my father and brothers came in to find out what was going on. I stood there thinking smugly that I was going to be told what a good child I was for handing the sweets in and having done as I was told.

Imagine my horror when my parents and brothers shared the sweets between them and ate them. I refused point blank to take even one, convinced they could be poisoned, and sat on the edge of the bed wondering with a six-year-old's logic, how long would it take before they all died.

I wasn't frightened, just curious.

WHITE

When I grew older, as well as the red-berried rowan trees, the ones that made the biggest impression on me were the large, white, horse chestnut trees that lined the drive leading up to Henbury Manor, which stood opposite our farm. Our two friends, the Formby boys, lived there with their parents and a baby brother who was too young to be of any interest, even to me who always loved babies. More interesting was the large Belgian Hare that lived in the courtyard ... it was huge.

The trees were in full bloom, it was a glorious day, and David, the two boys and I were idly walking up the drive, hoping that maybe biscuits might be on offer. David spotted something lying in the grass under a tree.

We gathered around, David declared it to be a dead body, and he poked 'it' with a stick.

'It' reared up, bellowing loudly; it was a tramp enjoying a welcome rest from his walk along the Dorchester road. You would have had to go a long way to find four children who could run faster than we did that day!

RED, WHITE and BLUE - Coronation

I can remember clearly, sitting in the classroom when the headmistress came to tell us that King George VI had died and that we would now have a queen. It was a trifle confusing to a class of eight-year-olds ... none of our teachers were taking much notice of us and there were a lot of red eyes and damp handkerchiefs amongst them that day.

In the weeks leading up to the Coronation during the following year, we were all painting Union Jacks with school paints and brushes. One girl, sitting next to me, had her own box of watercolours, which contained Prussian blue, rather than the usual ultramarine. Prussian blue seemed a strange colour to me, so totally different, and her painting looked a bit odd. Now it is my favourite blue ... sharp and strong.

Sketch above done in 2012

Not everyone in 1953 had a TV set, we didn't, but I was lucky enough to be invited to spend Coronation day with a school friend, Margaret, and her family, watching the outside broadcast on their black and white set.

Having watched the images of royalty, carriages, the crowds and the ceremony itself, I decided to paint a picture of all the people in a crowd scene. I was very proud when my painting was hung in the school entrance hall, that is until I heard one of the older girls say, "Huh, the people don't have any necks!"

BROWN

I've belonged to Romsey Art Group for over 43 years now ... it could be over 45, but I can't remember which daughter was a baby when I joined. In 2012, the RAG held a special celebratory exhibition, depicting some of the events that had taken place since Queen Elizabeth II came to the throne.

My given subject was 'the Coronation', and I chose to portray a family, along with their neighbours, watching a small black and white TV. Even the Corgi is captivated by the spectacle.

I have included a Chelsea Pensioner, to represent the passing of time. He is reading his newspaper, which contains the breaking news of the conquest of Everest, which was the other top story of the day.

There are two neighbours sitting on the sofa; the lady sipping sherry, who could have been one of my mother's assorted friends, and the man smoking a cigar and holding an ashtray, who is based on a friend of Granddad's, known to us three children as 'Bill'.

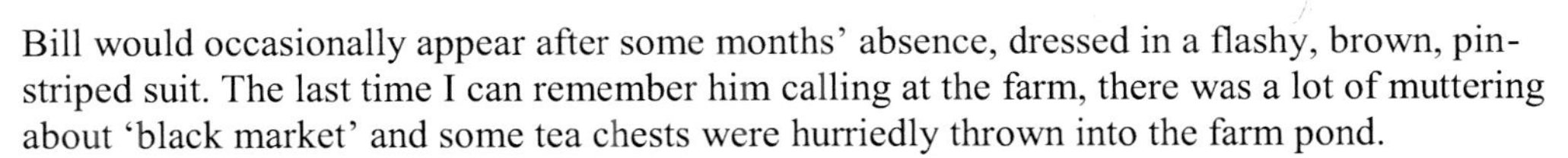

Bill would occasionally appear after some months' absence, dressed in a flashy, brown, pin-striped suit. The last time I can remember him calling at the farm, there was a lot of muttering about 'black market' and some tea chests were hurriedly thrown into the farm pond.

YELLOW and BLACK

My balance has always been poor, but I finally learned to ride a bicycle at the ripe old age of thirteen, and as a 'reward' my father bought me an old second-hand bike, which I promptly painted in yellow and black stripes.

It was suggested that I was now capable of riding my bike to school, a journey of two miles.

I was not a good cyclist and could only keep my balance if I was signalling that I was turning left.

Fortunately, the route consisted of left hand turns.

It was a relief when I cycled home on my last day at school and abandoned the now silver and pink bike in the coal shed, never to be used by me again.

I think my brothers may have taken it to pieces, as they had with the one and only doll's pram that I was given many years before, turning it into a sort of go-kart.

On the next page is my painting inspired by Radio Solent's report of 'Naked Bike Ride Day, 2011'.

Apparently, five naked bike rides were going to take place that day, to draw attention to the dangers of bike riding and how people just don't notice cyclists. I'm sure they did that day!

The following September, Richard Cartridge of Radio Solent, opened our annual Woodlanders Exhibition in Burley. He also invited five of us to join him in the studio for his Sunday afternoon broadcast, asking us each to take a piece of work with us, to talk about.

THE NAKED BIKE RIDE

On the Naked Bike Ride day, one of the five events was in our locality. As the weather that day was rather chilly, I dare say the bike riders didn't look their best.

It made me think of my first day at art school, when having just come from an all-girls school, and even though I had two brothers and we weren't exactly a prudish family, it came as a bit of a shock to be expected to draw the thin, wrinkled old gentleman sitting there in all his glory. Over the years we had many more models and I enjoyed the discipline of life drawing.

It was with a little trepidation that we accepted Richard Cartridge's invitation to Radio Solent. Brian Williams talked about his woodcarving, Carole Dickson about her pottery, and Tony Mercier, Brian Harrild and I spoke about our paintings.

Richard had requested that I took the 'Naked Bike Ride' with me and it proved to be rather difficult to politely describe on radio!

A FINE BALANCE

Another challenge to me is going out in boats … funny because I love to paint boats, but I really prefer them to be in the harbour.

This was always a bit of a disappointment to Ted, my husband, with his nautical background. Believe me, I try, but I still can't help my knees turning to jelly.

When our son Ben was about fourteen, Ted decided on a nostalgic visit to Poole Park that it would be 'fun' to take a rowing boat onto the lake and then he could give Ben a rowing lesson. So far, so good … the problem arose when Ben and Ted had to change places, making the boat rock and me panic. I hysterically insisted they immediately row me to the side of the lake where I could disembark. This they did. I stepped onto land, and it was only then that I realised that, had I wished, I could have just climbed out of the boat and walked to 'safety' … the lake was only a few inches deep.

CADMIUM YELLOW and OLIVE GREEN

My mother was always keen on having her hair coloured and cut well, and as she did not drive, my father used to take her to the salon and return later to collect her. Sometimes the to-ing and fro-ing was a bit of a problem, with the all-too-short afternoon closing time of the pub.

After a visit from her cousin Leon, a well-known hair stylist in Dublin, a package arrived from him. It was some special treatment for creating hi-lights, the idea being that with a bit of help from a willing friend the hi-lights could be put on at home.

The present arrived on a Saturday morning and by Sunday afternoon my mother could no longer contain her excitement, so I was 'press ganged' into helping her, and was told it would 'save so much time'.

I had never done anything like this before and was very reluctant. With the aid of bowls, spatulas, water, cotton wool, and the powder, etc., the 'goo' was applied and left on for the instructed time. But when the goo was washed off, my mother's hair of dark blonde was full of straight yellow stripes, like a blonde zebra.

Rather than be upset by this, she declared, "Ah well, it really is a lovely colour. Why not do the whole of my head?"

You didn't argue with my mother when she was determined about anything. Under orders, I applied the rest of the contents in the bowl. The end result was the same colour as the yellow trolley buses that used to run in Bournemouth … for those who can't remember them, they were BRIGHT CADMIUM YELLOW.

This second attempt brought on an attack of hysteria (for both of us) and my father forbade my mother to set one foot in the bar that night.

The following morning my Aunt Zona took my mother, wearing a large headscarf, to the salon, desperate for Roger, my mother's pet hair stylist, to 'do something'.

The best he could do was OLIVE GREEN, and a very unflattering short haircut. Poor Mummy!

When it came for our eldest daughter, Kait, to leave school, she was adamant that she had no intention of going to college.

We were living in rural Wiltshire at the time and there weren't that many jobs for young people. Knowing how much money my mother, 'Granny Barbara', had spent over the years at the hairdressers, my father said to Kait, "Why don't you go in for hairdressing? You will always be able to earn a living, as most women would commit murder to have their hair done."

His words, recalling my mother's attitude to the subject, had a ring of truth in them.

This particular painting is based on all sorts of things Kait has told us, and portrays her working in a salon. A lady is having hi-lights properly done, another is having her nails manicured, a young man is sitting under the hair dryer having a perm, and another client is undecided about what she wants. The one thing that makes me laugh is Kait's comment, "When sitting in a salon chair, the larger the client, the wider the knees."

PRIMROSE and OLIVE

Cows are one of my all-time favourite animals, and they are certainly NOT stupid, as some people believe. My grandfather, Ted Burry, had a dairy herd of some sixty Ayrshire cows, and he later added some Friesians to the herd to improve the quality of milk. There were two milking sheds in the farmyard and as the cows came through the gate to the yard, each cow turned and walked to her own place.

Granddad had lost his earlier milking herd during WW II to foot and mouth disease, when instead of burning, a large lime pit was dug. It must have been heart-breaking, and ten years later, the only thing Grandad could do with the particular field was to cut the grass.

Apart from the dairy herd there was Primrose, the Jersey house cow, who could at times behave like one! When my grandparents, my aunt Olive and Great Aunt Ethel moved to Brockenhurst, leaving my father to run Henbury Farm, Primrose remained with us for a while.

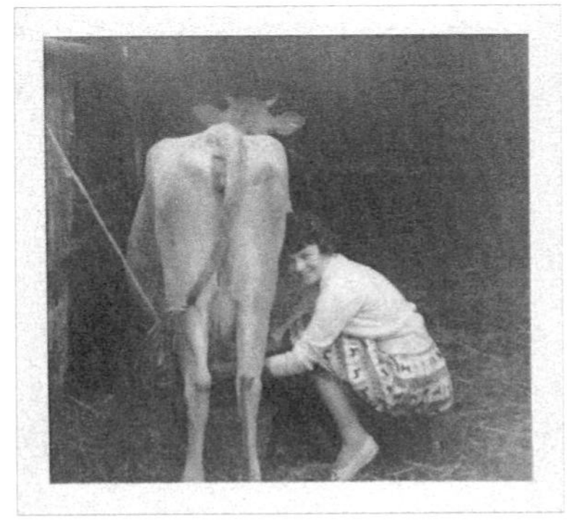

My father found milking Primrose a trifle awkward with his large man's hands, so in the absence of Olive, I was given the job to do before and after school. On a summer afternoon it was relaxing to lean against her as she stood to be milked. She smelt of warm lanolin and sunshine.

She could be a bit of a madam though – her tail had to be tied out of the way, as she had a way of whipping whoever was in charge of the milk pail around the face. If you avoided that, then she would suddenly cough loudly and her udders would fly out of your hands. She also had a way of literally 'kicking the bucket'.

Before long, Primrose moved to Brockenhurst in the New Forest and was reunited with Olive. The painting on the opposite page shows them surrounded by some of Granny's 'fowls', who always seemed to be there, scratching about, along with a couple of hopeful farmyard cats.

When Primrose neared the end of her working life, Granddad put her in a field near Whitley Ridge, along with some of his ponies, to enjoy her retirement. She was quite happy until the morning when Granddad went to check all was well with the animals and found Primrose had died during the night, following a heavy thunderstorm. Her memory lives on – what a cow!

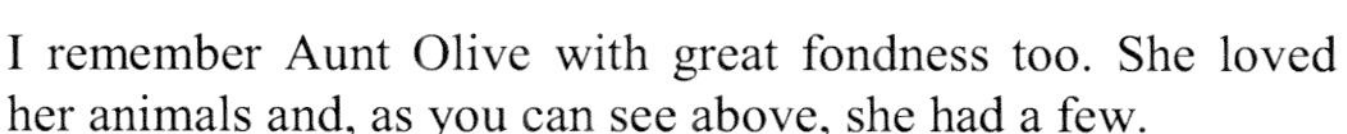

I remember Aunt Olive with great fondness too. She loved her animals and, as you can see above, she had a few.

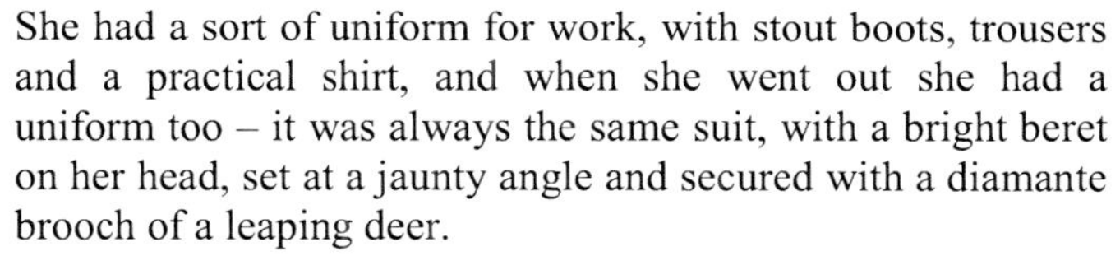

She had a sort of uniform for work, with stout boots, trousers and a practical shirt, and when she went out she had a uniform too – it was always the same suit, with a bright beret on her head, set at a jaunty angle and secured with a diamante brooch of a leaping deer.

When snow has fallen during the night, the farmer brings a welcome feed of hay out to his hungry cows.

Again Primrose is centre stage, and is she suggesting to the busy chickens that they leave the hay alone and concentrate on their own food in the trough?

TAKING THE COW TO MARKET

Growing up on a farm, our childhood games could be a trifle basic and earthy.

When it was too wet or cold to play outside, Paul, 11, David, 8 – a year younger than me, and I, had a game of our own invention.

It was called 'Taking the Cow to Market'.

All it involved was the old chintz settee that dominated the living room, a stick and we three children.

Paul always took the part of the lorry driver, driving at reckless speed. David was the cow and suffered from noisy stomach problems, and I was the cowman who wielded the stick – a role played with gusto.

What delightful children we were!

Recently, on a birthday with a big '0' in it, Paul drew me a sketch book, charting my life.

In his book was the picture opposite – please excuse the language!

About fifteen years ago at a family gathering, we decided, with the aid of a liquid lunch, to re-enact our childhood game for the 'enjoyment' of our respective families. David had grown into a rather large chap, Paul had much more dignity, having spent many, many years in the Army, but I must admit that I played my role as before.

Our assortment of wives, husbands, children and grandchildren were absolutely horrified and find it difficult to talk about to this day.

THE FOWELL FAMILY AT HOME

Sofas often feature in my family scenes, I particularly like the over-stuffed variety, worn into particular comfy shapes by constant heavy use.

Many years ago there was a TV programme hosted by Noel Edmunds, called 'Lucky Numbers', and every so often he would invite people to send in drawings depicting a list of things to be included. On one occasion he suggested; a TV, chains clanking, a child crying, a dog barking, a radio playing and a couple of other things that I can't recall.

I sent in my drawing and it was shown the following week, along with many from other people. I then thought about my drawing and decided to develop the idea into a family 'at home' amidst all sorts of domestic chaos.

The teenager wearing flares (so you can tell how long ago it was) is our daughter Kait, and she is trying to listen to HER music. The mother is reading what my grandmother would have called 'a penny dreadful', i.e. a trashy magazine, and the father is asleep, doing his impersonation of a couch potato.

A child is lying on the floor having worked out her maths homework on her leg with a felt tip pen, and the only ones paying any attention to the most unsuitable programme on the TV, are the dog and a baby on a potty.

I hasten to add that it is not a portrayal of our family.

GRANDDAD BURRY

Granddad, my father's father, features in so many of my country and farm paintings, dressed in his breeches, boots, waistcoats and collarless striped shirts, which were sometimes adorned with a neckerchief. In the winter he would wear a tweed cap and in the summer a battered off-white hat, similar to the type a cricket umpire might wear.

When he sat in the old leather armchair, buttoning up his highly polished gaiters, I was intrigued. He was quite a picture too when he entered the show ring with one of his beautiful ponies or horses.

The Burrys had farmed in the Christchurch area as far back as it is possible to remember. According to one aged document, a Burry girl was given a piece of land near where the famous 'Cat and Fiddle' now stands, as her dowry back in the 1600s. (One maybe unknown fact is that the 'Cat and Fiddle' was the last pub in the area to be granted a 7 day licence, back in the 1950s.)

Granddad spent all his life dairy farming and breeding racehorses and New Forest ponies, for which he and his daughter, Olive, were well known and respected. Olive's mare, 'Dolly Grey IX', was 'New Forest Show Supreme Champion' at the first New Forest Show after the war, in 1949.

Granddad and Olive sold many of the New Forest ponies to the Scandinavians when they were starting their own herds in the 1950s.

Suzan, age three, on Dolly Grey IX

Granddad, Albert Edward Burry, or 'Ted Burry' as he was known, was born into a farming family from in and around Christchurch and Mudeford, and as the eldest of three, he was encouraged to leave school as soon as he was old enough to start work on the farm. He told me once, that as a young boy it was his job to take the stallion on walkabout to various farms and obliging mares.

In the photograph below, Granddad Burry is about eight years old at a family wedding in about 1900, sitting with an assortment of aunts, uncles and cousins, outside what was 'The New Lodge', in Somerford, now no longer in existence having been knocked down in the name of progress.

In the photograph are Farwells, Bartletts and Burrys, the three families being closely connected, having made more than one marriage between them.

Granddad was a very shrewd, 'careful' man, and quite a character. I was told the following tale by the owner of a large intimidating bull, when he drove me to visit my stepmother in Southampton Hospital. Mary had fallen, breaking her hip, on Christmas Eve and spent Christmas Day being 'mended'.

Apparently, my companion had received a phone call from the Balmer Lawn Hotel, asking if a bull, who was glaring through the window at breakfasting hotel guests, could possibly be his.

He lives on the far side of Brockenhurst, so he drove over, and yes, it was his bull. But there was no way he could get the animal in the car, so he thought, 'Ah-ha, Mr Burry's yard is just round the corner, I'll walk the bull down to him and ask if he could keep an eye on him while I go to fetch some suitable transport.'

All went well. Granddad was in the yard cleaning out, and in one of the stalls was Primrose, the house cow. She was in season, which meant the A.I. (the artificial insemination people) would need to be contacted … at quite a cost to Granddad. Granddad must have thought it was his lucky day. He readily agreed, saying, "Yes, I'll take care of him until you get back. No need to hurry, I might have a little job for him."

Granny and Granddad were the first in the family to have a television, renting it as people did in those days, from an electrical shop here in Burley. The sole purpose for the TV was to watch the horse racing in the afternoons, and woe betide anyone who interrupted their viewing. I am not sure where they laid their bets, but they did quite well and were very knowledgeable about the horses.

Racing was so important to Granny and Olive. My husband, Ted, and I took our tiny daughter Kait to meet them when she was just a few weeks old and we had to sit quietly until the race that they were watching was over. Granddad came into the room as we sat there, looked at his new great granddaughter and said, "Looks like a good do-er," – a compliment from Granddad.

My father's sisters, Olive and Rene, said that my father was Granny's favourite, which could have been true, they even shared the same birthday, June 13th, and my father was named after one of Granny's numerous brothers.

GRANNY BURRY

Granny was born 'Ivy Bartlett', on 13th June 1891, into a farming family from Hurn village, and attended the village school with her siblings. She told me once that there were about forty children at the school and only four surnames. Granny met Granddad at Ringwood market and they were married in 1911, and settled down at Mudeford Farm, near Christchurch, where they stayed, until moving to Henbury Farm, Sturminster Marshall, Dorset, just before the start of WW II.

She was not the sort of farmer's wife to get involved with the larger animals, leaving that side of things to Granddad, my father and aunts, Rene and Olive, although I do remember her salting down the odd pig. Granny, with the help of Great Aunt Ethel, whom we all called 'Auntie', ran the house, and provided large meals for everyone.

The enormous teapot, brought out at every meal, was a legend in itself. It used to sit, wearing a large tea cosy, in pride of place on top of one of Granny's ancient tablecloths. The table itself seemed enormous to me as a child, with the whole family around it, plus anyone else who might be calling, even Fatty Haysom, the baker from Sturminster Marshall.

In 1952 Granny and Granddad, along with Olive and Auntie, moved to Brockenhurst, and my parents, with we three children in tow, moved into Henbury Farm. The original farmhouse at Brockenhurst, that belonged to the land that Granddad bought, backed onto the sewage works, and for once Granny had her way ... she would NOT live in the house. Granddad kept the land, sold the house and the stables to other people, and bought a house for Granny further down the road. A newly married couple bought the stables, turning it into a cosy home. Many, many years later, when my parents were divorced, my father met the lady who had bought the stables with her now ex-husband, and Mary and my father were married.

Granny's hair was once raven black, but by the time we came along it had turned white and was worn in a neat bun at the nape of her neck. She had enormous big brown eyes and was quite tall. The family height comes from Granny – all her grandsons and great grandsons, are over six foot tall. Out of all her granddaughters and great granddaughters I am the shortest. I take after my mother.

I loved the look of Granny.

Granny, Aunt Rene, Elizabeth, Suzan and Olive

On her head she wore either a knitted, navy blue, pull-on woollen hat or, on the odd occasion when she was taken out in the car, she would wear a navy blue, straw hat with a wide brim. She always wore navy blue dresses with lacy collars, a navy blue cardigan and, over the top of all this, a floral cross-over overall, which was removed late in the afternoon, after she fed 'the fowls'.

It was at this stage that she would sit down in the front room and wait until she saw Primrose, the cow, having spent the day on the Forest, walk past the hedge and into the yard to be milked. Granny would then get up to lay the table and prepare yet another large tea, with lashings of bread and butter and cake. Instead of jam, Aunt Olive preferred to cut up a tomato and lace it with vinegar and pepper, enough to make the eyes of anyone sitting next to her, water.

Granny was the one who did the washing and ironing, using two flat irons that she heated on the range, and spitting delicately to see if they were hot enough. It has always been a family joke that Granny's washing line looked like a wind sock convention on washday. Granny, Auntie, and Aunt Olive all wore pastel-coloured Directoire knickers, commonly referred to as 'D.Ks', 'apple stealers' or 'harvest festivals' (all safely gathered in).

During our last holiday to West Bay, on a lousy, cold, wet, summer's day, we ended up making a short bus journey into Bridport. Ted and Sophie went their own way, and I took my twelve-year-old granddaughter, Georgi, and eight-year-old grandson, Joe, into the Arts Centre to see an exhibition by the local art group. It's always interesting to look at other people's work.

Our next port of call was the Bridport Museum, where a very patient lady was helping visiting children to make peg dolls with all sorts of lace, paper, ribbons and glue. Georgi wandered off and discovered a room full of Victorian clothing. She was delighted to discover that she could go through the rails and try the clothes and bonnets on. Imagine her reaction when she found an enormous pair of long legged cotton bloomers and asked me if they were the sort her great, great grandmother wore. I didn't like to mention that in their day such garments were considered quite risqué, even though she was laughing at them for being so old-fashioned.

EDWARD GEORGE BURRY my father

My parents, Barbara Brandon and Edward (George) Burry, married in 1939 against the advice of my father's doctors, who were concerned that he hadn't fully recovered from his serious flying accident.

Over the next five years, Paul, then me, and then David, were born. Neither parent was a great disciplinarian, but so long as we obeyed Daddy's 'golden rules' of table manners, politeness, bedtimes and no bad language, all went relatively smoothly – although for a while he was backing a loser on the last one as far as I went. Paul was at school, David a small toddler, and I was in Auntie Rene's company for a lot of the time, But when she was helping with showing ponies or horses, or had gone racing, I was left in the tender care of the dairyman and his wife, and to say they had a colourful vocabulary would be putting it mildly.

Like all small children I picked up things that I shouldn't, but I learnt in time from the glowering looks by Daddy, that it was not acceptable, although I kept it in reserve for dealing with my brothers. Daddy told me off one day for saying, 'ave, and I went into my bedroom and wrote 'AV' on my blackboard, thinking I was being really naughty.

Daddy and our granddad, although they respected each other, didn't have a lot in common, apart from a love of horses. Daddy was complex, sometimes moody, and he could be very eccentric in his dress, sporting colourful bow ties and shirts. He loved the theatre, books, music, films, art … and us. He was also a good amateur actor.

Because of Mummy's enforced hospital stay and long recovery from TB, he took on a lot of our mother's roles. He was the one that took us to the doctors, the dentist, the hairdressers, to school, to buy our shoes and school uniforms, and still he worked hard on the farm.

From his early 20s until his late 30s he was a National Hunt jockey, and only retired when he broke his left collar bone, not for the first time, and was told that it would be dangerous if he was to damage it again in the future.

He was put in a plaster jacket for a few weeks, which caused a few problems, as we children racing around would knock his elbow, causing him to break one of his 'golden rules'.

Daddy would take us out in the car on a Sunday afternoon – that is if we three could agree where we wanted to go. David liked Badbury Rings, Paul preferred Poole Park, possibly because there was a miniature steam train running on a track in the park, but I would go for Sandbanks, as I loved building castles and moats. We would be asked, "Well where is it to be ?" … and we would argue of course. We never learnt, and at that point he would say, "Right you wotsits, if you can't decide peacefully, you are not going anywhere." With that he would pick up the newspaper and go into the garage to sit in the car, reading or, as I suspect, snoozing.

David's started to Hum!
I hate Poole Park!
David's let off!
We always go where Paul wants!
Percy's eating my book!
Sandbanks makes me Sick!
I want to go to Blandford!

None of you Buggers is going anywhere!

I am sure it was all too much for him at times, but there was usually someone living with us to help. I have fond memories of a series of girls and their babies from an unmarried mothers home in Poole, who used to come to us for six months or so after their babies were born, and stay with us until they decided what they were going to do with their lives.

When we moved to 'The Stocks Inn' our Sunday visits continued, but now it was often to the Pitt Rivers Museum, near Cranborne. We all enjoyed that, most of all Daddy. I would stand with him, looking at the glass cases full of tiny figures set out to represent Roman burial grounds … more patterns. Another destination he was happy to go to was Kingston Lacy House, which in those days was only opened on an occasional Sunday. Daddy was as interested in the wonderful art collection as I was. It had been Mummy's idea to move to The Stocks, but I'm not sure if Daddy really liked being 'mine host', although we were there for eleven years.

When Ted and I were married, Daddy decided to move to Brockenhurst to help his elderly parents and sister Olive, as by that time he and Mummy were divorced. After four years he married Mary Penny, a lady who lived near the family and often assisted Olive in the show ring, and who was as different from Mummy as anyone could be.

Three months before we moved to Burley, I had my first solo exhibition at the Salisbury Arts Centre, and was looking forward to my father and Mary coming to the Preview. The day before the preview he phoned me to say he was unwell, but never mind, he was certain there would be another exhibition and he promised to be there. Sadly that was not to be. He died a few weeks later, just before we moved. He is buried in Brockenhurst cemetery, along with the rest of our family.

BARBARA BRANDON my mother

My mother, Barbara, was lovely to look at and a bubbly, fun-loving person, never seeming to take life too seriously, although I am sure she did at times. She encouraged us all to see the funny side of things, and luckily, all four of us, my brothers, Paul, David and Robin, and I, have been born with a sense of the ridiculous, helping us through life.

Mummy didn't like school, getting her sister, Zona, to forge letters, supposedly from their mother, saying she was too ill to attend, and then they would spend long summer days on the beach at Southbourne, where they lived, making home movies with their friends. The actor who became Stewart Granger wanted to join in, but for some reason they wouldn't let him.

Mummy was only 21 when her own mother died, but Daddy's family thought the world of her and bore her no grudge when she and our father divorced some 24 years later.

Barbara (Mummy) with her mother at the farm

When Granny knew she had remarried and had a new baby, my brother Robin, she invited them to visit, letting her know she understood, even though my father was always 'the apple of her eye'. I think Auntie Rene missed Mummy though when she moved away, as they had been good friends.

Mummy enjoyed breeding dogs, her garden, and people. Everyone loved her, and when we were at The Stocks it was her, as landlady, that people came to see. She was fun to be with and would be the first to forgive any misdemeanour.

We all caused her the odd headache as we were growing up, especially me as I was very stubborn, more like Daddy, but she and I became very close in her later years when Robin, Kait, Sophie and Ben were growing up.

David, Barbara, Paul, George and Suzan Burry - 1945

Mummy used to say she wasn't artistic, but if you gave her a room full of odds and ends, pieces of furniture, paintings, pots, etc., within a few hours she would turn it into a welcoming, comfortable, unusual place ... a useful talent as my parents moved home many times.

When I was small she would scribble on a plain piece of paper, and then encourage me to fill in the spaces with colour and patterns. Little did she know she was starting me off on an approach that I still use today ... and she was the one that gave her blessing for me to go to art school.

Mummy loved animals and entered wholeheartedly into the country pursuits and shows that were part of our family's yearly activities.

Here she is 'studying form' at a local point to point at Morden, near Sturminster Marshall.

From the left – David, Paul, George, three fellow Dorset farmers, Barbara and Suzan.

A couple of weeks before Ted and I married, and with the advice of our uncle Jack, who said Mummy had every right to be at the wedding, it was arranged for Daddy, Mummy and stepfather Ken, to meet on mutual ground, as they hadn't spoken since the divorce. Ted and I were at the meeting as referees … if needed. We weren't, and Daddy even complimented Mummy on her baby, Robin.

Ken, Barbara and Kait

Daddy remarried and for a while he, Mary, Mummy and Ken would meet at family occasions, but Mary didn't really understand how we could all be so 'civilised', and made her excuses.

Never having been strong, Mummy died at the age of sixty, leaving Ken and fourteen-year-old Robin. At the get together after the cremation, Ken and Daddy got quietly drunk together.

I am grateful to my parents for showing me that there is no point in carrying around grudges, it's all a waste of time, life is too short. Whenever Mummy is spoken about, it is always with affection.

THE STOCKS INN

Granny, Auntie Olive, Auntie Rene and Lizzie, but NOT Granddad, would occasionally go out for rides in Granddad's car on a summer's afternoon and sometimes they would call to see us at The Stocks. Never, ever, did they venture into the bar, but Granny would have one little tipple on these visits ... just the one, a gin and peppermint. Auntie Olive, and Lizzie, my small cousin, would have lemonade and crisps, while Rene kept Granny company, in the back seat of the old battered Austin, sipping away at her glass of stout.

As in all country pubs, animals were always welcomed – we all loved them, but it was not without mishap when the dogs owned by Mr Bill Isaacs attacked one of our cats, Boozer.

It was at the fireplace shown in this photo of Bill Issacs, that we would sit having a little relaxation on a Sunday afternoon. Before 'all day' opening hours, a pub would open from 10am until 2.30pm and then close, to reopen at 6pm until 10.30pm, or 11pm in the summer. Sunday was different, opening at 12 noon to allow people to go to church, and then closing at 2pm. The Sunday evening hours were 7pm until 10pm, and the 'long' Sunday afternoons gave publicans and their families a bit of a break.

One wintery afternoon, Mummy and I were sitting close up to the fire in the public bar, trying to ignore the draughts from windows and doors. Daddy was upstairs at his desk doing his accounts for the week, and I am not sure where the boys were. The desk 'lived' in a double-doored cupboard, just above the said bar.

Suddenly a loud shot rang out. "Oh my goodness," shrieked my mother, "Your father has shot himself. Go and look!" ... which I reluctantly did, only to find him at his desk, holding the revolver that he kept in one of the desk drawers. He looked a bit shocked and said he had just been looking at it and hadn't realised it was loaded. The bullet had not only just missed Mummy and me, but it had made a hole in the ceiling.

"What will we say if anyone asks what that hole is?" Mummy wondered. "Oh, I know, I will say I was sweeping the floor after closing time and the broom handle went up into the ceiling."

Daddy looked at her and said, "I don't think they will believe it, maybe the bit about the handle doing the damage, but certainly not the bit about you sweeping the floor."
Just another day at The Stocks Inn!

Whether there was any truth in this or not, I am not sure, but my mother and some of her friends who frequented the pub, did firmly believe it. In the late 1950s there were only two bars at The Stocks, the public bar, and a small private bar where my mother reigned supreme. When she and just a few customers were in the little bar on a cold, dark, windy evening, the door to the small car park would suddenly fly open for no reason and there would be no one there.

Our own Halloween ghost in stocks.

One of our ancient locals told her that it was the ghost of a man who had committed murder back in the 1920s. This man had been with his wife and her parents in their farmhouse at Walford, just as you come out of Wimborne on the Cranborne road. What really happened no one knew, but the man ended up shooting not only his wife, but his in-laws as well. He made his way up to The Stocks, where at that time his brother was the landlord, and banged on the door, trying to get in for sanctuary, without success. He went into a nearby field and shot himself. The ghostly opening of the door was believed to be the guilty man trying to get in … who knows?

A few months before we moved from Henbury Farm to The Stocks Inn, a brood mare came to us, but sadly died having her foal. Even though the foal had a famous sire, the owner did not want him as his leg had been damaged during the traumatic birth and he would never be capable of racing. The owner virtually disowned him, so my mother decided to hand rear the poor foal. A companion for him, another orphan, was found, this time a New Forest foal whose mother had been killed by a car in the Forest.

Throughout the summer both foals appeared to thrive and enjoyed each other's company, but sadly 'Hop-a-long', as the thoroughbred foal had been named, died shortly before we moved. There were stables at The Stocks and we took the now extremely cheeky New Forest foal with us. He was becoming too 'tame' and liked to come into the bar looking for treats from the customers, so in time a new home was found for him as he needed someone who could spend a lot of time convincing him he was a pony, not a human.

A lady called 'Mrs Taylor' was so good to us at The Stocks, but she would never have dreamt of setting foot behind the bar. We children being under eighteen were not allowed to serve alcohol or work in the bar, so when extra help was needed Hyla Stroud came to the rescue, working alongside my father in the public bar at the weekends and when we had darts matches.

Hyla was a neighbour of Mrs Taylor. He had been born in a cluttered cottage in the village, one of a large brood of children, and after a spell in the Royal Marines he returned to the same cottage and became a 'Jack of all Trades' – indispensable to many.

He was tall, very dapper and funny, and was a co-owner of Cindy, the pampered pooch who suffered at the paws of Percy and Gertie.

Suzan and Hyla Stroud

THE SWORDSMAN

My mother had been the landlady in four different pubs, and in all of them the customers loved her – a hard act to follow.

Taking a pub was the last thing I had wanted to do when growing up, but the opportunity presented itself and Ted and I became the tenants of 'The Swordsman' on our daughter Sophie's third birthday, December 12th 1972. What a time to take on this venture, just a couple of weeks before Christmas … and to make matters worse, both Sophie and her elder sister, Kait, went down with German measles on Boxing Day, needing the doctor, who was not too happy about leaving his family party for our spotty children.

When we took over the pub, in the village of Dinton, it was called 'East End Inn' and had been under Ushers Brewery ownership. Ted had collected knives, swords, and daggers for many years, and we displayed these behind the bar, safely attached to the walls and ceiling (it would not be allowed these days, what with health and safety) and because of the interesting collection, the pub's new owners, Watneys, allowed us to rename it 'The Swordsman'.

At first the pub had three small bars, but we knew full well that Watneys intended to turn it all into one large bar. Even so, for the first few months we ran the three bars – a small snug, a public bar and, in the middle, a 'Jug and Bottle'.

The 'Jug and Bottle' was an off license and was used mainly by people who didn't want to be seen drinking in a pub. They would scurry in with a container of some sort, we would fill it, and then they would hurry off home. More than one courting couple would use this little bar as a trysting place, as they wanted privacy, away from fathers and brothers, who were probably playing darts in the public bar.

Ted and I found the character of the pub changed, possibly for the better, once the alterations were complete, as it was now a much more open, friendly place, but some of the old timers didn't agree. It was then much easier to run, sometimes just needing one of us to be in the bar at a time, while the other could be with the children in our small living room that was just off the bar. Most of the time Ted and I ran the pub on our own, but we did have a few stalwarts who would step in when asked, including Laurie and Gwen, ex-licensees, who when not behind the bar, sat on the other side and supported us in other ways.

We were lucky with The Swordsman, it was a real village pub and as well as helping Ted running it, I was able to give the children the attention they needed, and do my painting. We spent more than twelve happy years there and still keep in touch with many 'old' customers from those days.

Nearly four years after taking on the pub, our son Ben was born. The year before I had been diagnosed with Type 1 diabetes, and I was told I was to spend the four weeks before he was born in Odstock Hospital. It was the hot summer of 1976 and the pub was extra busy with thirsty, hot villagers. Fortunately, my mother-in-law, Kit, was living opposite us, having moved to be near us when my father-in-law died, and she offered help.

Kit was wonderful, looking after Kait and Sophie, preparing food and washing glasses, but not going into the bar.

They all managed well, as I lazed around getting larger and larger by the minute. All went as planned and Ben was born on August 4th. For many years, when on that day the National Anthem was played first thing on the radio on the Queen Mother's birthday, he thought it was for him!

In all I spent seven weeks at Odstock Hospital – the initial four weeks before Ben was born then the usual eight days recuperation, after which we went home for a week, where I had an awful 'hypo' and went into a coma, which meant going back to Odstock for a further week for my insulin to be adjusted, and because Ben was so young he returned with me.

Ted and I felt that we would like to repay some of the kindness and care that we had received, and over the years we would arrange an event of some sort to raise funds for the children's ward at the hospital.

Jubilee Football fundraising match, May 7th 1977 'Queens' versus 'Slack Alices'

Standing: Ted, John Lee, Richard Bull, Derek Johnson, Frank Coombes, John Burgess, Alan Lee, Malcolm King, Sandy, Mike Frampton, Roy Booth. Squatting in front: John Avery & ?

One of our first fund raising ideas was a charity football match, and many of our customers, both girls and boys, men and women, gave it their 'blessing', forming two teams – 'The Queens' and 'The Slack Alices'. I'm not sure which team was which, but the 'ladies' wore their T-shirts and shorts, and the 'men', including my husband Ted, were in drag. Ted's outfit was a navy blue Crimplene frock, padded out with two large balloons. On his head he sported one of his mother's favourite creations, and on his feet he wore ankle socks and big boots. The look on his face in this photo says it all.

There didn't appear to be any rules in the game and it was declared a draw, of course.

A tidy sum was made on that occasion, and with the help of one of our customers, Richard, and his connection with Tesco's, we were able to take all sorts of Christmas presents up to the Children's Ward, to share between the children, some of whom were going to be in hospital for a long time.

SUE THE SIOUX

One of our customers, Brian, was a coach driver, and was friends with a fellow called 'Geoff Ridout' who was involved with running a Native American village at Dodington House, near Bristol.

Geoff's Sioux name was 'Spotted Eagle' and he was the son of a full-blooded Sioux G.I., who came to England in World War II and stayed, marrying a local girl.

We arranged for Geoff to come to The Swordsman with his sons, all decked out in traditional costume. Our children and their friends dressed up too and it was a great sight.

Spotted Eagle entertained us, telling us about tribal behaviour and the rules in daily life.

Knowing I painted, he explained how the use of colour on their teepees follows a strict pattern, and he asked me to design some drawings for him that could be sold. It was a very successful evening, and again we were able to support the children at Odstock.

To repay the compliment of Geoff's family's visit, Ted arranged a coach trip to see the Native American village.

Off we went one Saturday morning, minus a few customers who had booked seats – I think over-enthusiasm at the previous night's darts match was the excuse. The rest of us had a great day, and to make it even better, Geoff made Ted, the children and me, 'Honorary Sioux'. If I felt so inclined I could call myself 'Sue the Sioux'! Don't worry, I can't hear your groans.

It was wonderful for Ted, who was always a keen Western movie fan. We were lucky to visit the village because it was only there for two years.

Darts matches – another regular feature at The Swordsman.

Running a pub was much less complicated when we were tenants; so long as we paid our rent and bought the beer etc. from the brewery, we were left to run our pub as we wanted. The era of managers and targets were just starting when we called it a day.

Our pub was like many village pubs – beer, spirits, darts, snacks, cribbage, a game of spoof, NO children under the age of 14, and until youngsters were 18, they had to have an adult with them. Mind you, many a blind eye was turned to the last rule. When we had The Swordsman, Ted would allow the 17 year olds in to play darts … there was nowhere else for them to go in the village, and their parents knew Ted would make sure they behaved.

The 'other side' of the bar, was an eye opener – alcohol can have a surprising effect on some people.

It was a good life in the pub, so long as you remembered to be a good listener and to forget things that you were told in confidence (a case of in one ear and out of the other), to keep a still tongue, and to keep smiling. I learnt the last lesson the evening after my mother sadly died. We had a darts match arranged in the pub and, as no one else was available, I had to help Ted, even though I felt awful. Our locals knew what had happened and were brilliant, but I heard one of the visiting team say, "Who is the miserable cow behind the bar?" … such is life!

BROTHERS

PAUL as the eldest, was the more sensible and thoughtful of we three, and liked to invent and make things. I remember him designing a run for his bantam hens, and after a lot of banging posts and stretching chicken wire, he stood back admiring his handiwork. The bantams weren't so impressed, as they took flight straight over the wire in the direction of the railway line that ran at the bottom of the garden.

He loved his books, and at one of his own birthday parties he went missing, only to be found on his bed reading his new book, oblivious to what we were up to. Paul was always called by his proper name, whereas David and I were referred to collectively as 'the little ones'. I use Paul's persona for painting long suffering, slightly confused, mad professor types. My contemporaries at school were quite envious of me for having an older brother, knowing our parents allowed me to go to parties and dances with him, so long as he kept an eye on me. I am not sure if he appreciated my company.

Having been in the Army Cadets, Paul decided to join the regular Army, where he remained for 27 years. When he retired from the Army, Euro Tunnel snapped him up, and finally he became an advisor on security, travelling widely.

After retiring again, and with their daughters, Birgit and Angela, settled, Paul and his wife, Erika, moved to Normandy, where he spends his time buying and renovating classic cars, building up a good wine cellar, and whizzing around on a 'ride on' lawn mower.

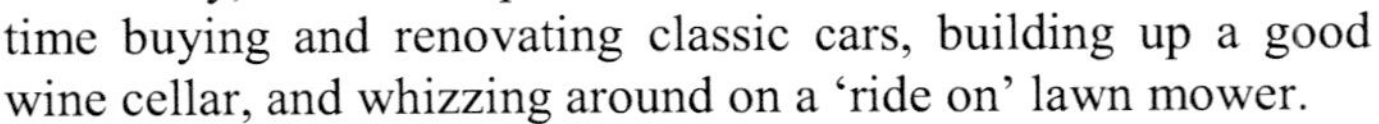

He is also a good cartoonist, and for my 70th birthday compiled a book for me, depicting some memories that we both share.

As children, my brothers never seemed to be very sympathetic, but judging from one of the cartoons Paul drew, he must have remembered feeling a little sorry for me when our mother's father and stepmother, whom I could not remember ever having seen before, turned up for my fourth birthday party.

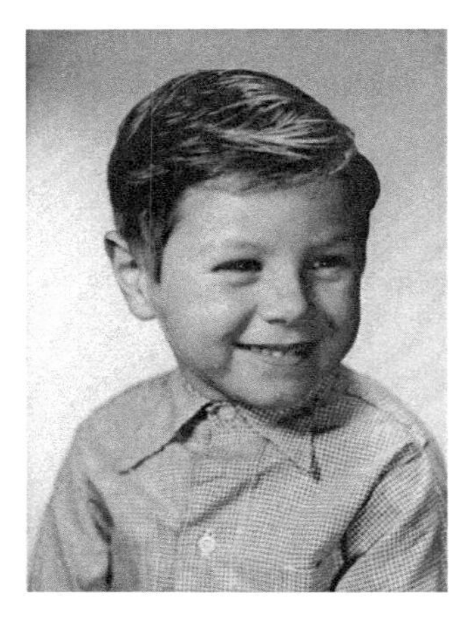

DAVID was, perhaps unfairly, considered the naughty one, being full of fun and daft ideas. He could get away with things that Paul and I couldn't. He would be forgiven and then go off and get up to some other scrape. He would have given William Brown a run for his money, and when painting cheeky boys I think of David.

He was not too keen on the classroom and loved any sport. He and his friends in the village spent their summer holidays messing about in the local river, and he became a very good swimmer, winning prizes at the school aqua-sports day many years running. His speciality was underwater swimming and, with his large chest, he was full of air ... or wind, another of his party tricks!

David loved his food and at the age of fourteen was more than a little overweight and no taller than me at 5 foot 2 inches. One afternoon David was showing off to his friends, riding on the tow bar of a tractor, annoying the driver, when he slipped. The roller behind the tractor went right over the top of him, but thankfully the ground was soft and that, in itself, saved his life. He managed to cycle home before being sent to hospital to have his inner thighs stitched up.

Suzan, aged about 17, with Paul and David

Our poor parents, they never knew what his next escapade would be. After his shocking experience, he started, quoting my brother, Paul, to 'grow upwards rather than outwards' and ended up at nearly six foot the following year.

David was always the last one to return home from school in the afternoons, and he would walk past the living window grinning, scruffy and minus his school cap, tie, and homework, explaining to our exasperated father that they had 'fallen out of the train window' ... again.

David married Julie, and their son, Ian, was born four months before Ted and I became the proud parents of Kait. Then their daughter, Zoe, was born four months after our second daughter, Sophie – another pattern.

Later he married Vicki, and when their boys, Oliver and James played rugby, David's love of the sport was more than evident – his loud voice could be heard above all others, shouting encouragement to all the team.

He worked hard all his life and was a bit of an entrepreneur. He loved a joke and, like our mother, never took life seriously and must have driven his patient wife, Vicki, to distraction. He was thoroughly enjoying being a grandfather when he sadly died, aged 66, surrounded by his family. He was smiling to the last.

OTHER GRANDPARENTS

Marie Lilian Hickisson Rushbrook and Louis Earle Badanski,

my mother's parents, were totally different from my father's farming family.

'Mummy's Mother', as Marie was called by us children (we never knew her as a 'granny'), had died of tuberculosis in 1941, six months after my eldest brother, Paul, was born.

She was one of thirteen children born to Isabella Clara Rushbrook and James Hickisson. When young, James had married a lady by the name of Elisabeth Bond, who was the only child of John Bond, the famous marking ink manufacturer, and they had two sons. Later, when he was about 55, he met eighteen-year-old Isabella, who at that time was a dancer/ actress, and they set up home together. In later documents James is described as the 'alleged' father of the thirteen children. He appears to have always supported them.

Isabella died at 39 in 1896, and James in 1897, well into his late 70s. The older children seemed to have taken care of the younger ones, but as they grew up they went their separate ways and very few kept in touch with each other. It is only thanks to a second cousin, Andy, and his wife, Pat, that I learned this much. Andy is the grandson of Nelson, one of Marie's brothers, and he and Pat researched the family history, making themselves known to me at a Woodlanders Exhibition. Andy and Pat have produced a whole file on the family, much of which was entirely unknown to my brothers and me.

In 1913, Marie, who we think was employed as a rep for a picture framer, met Louis, who at that time was making a living as a portrait painter. They fell in love and eloped. As Marie and Louis were of different faiths, and in view of opposition from their families, it seemed the easiest thing to do.

Louis was one of four children born to Sarah and Simeon Badanski, and they originated from an area of Poland that was under Russian control. He had two brothers, Maurice and Saul, and a sister, Rachael. Maurice went to live in Dublin, Saul to New York, but Rachael stayed at home and never married.

Marie and Louis married in 1914 and my aunt Zona was born in 1915, in Leeds. My mother, Barbara, followed in 1920, again in Leeds.

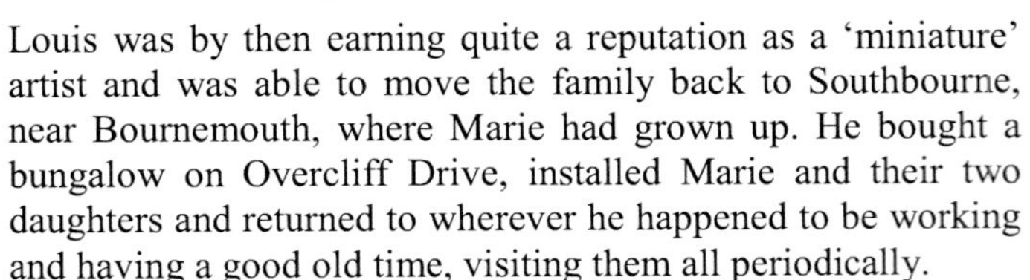

Louis was by then earning quite a reputation as a 'miniature' artist and was able to move the family back to Southbourne, near Bournemouth, where Marie had grown up. He bought a bungalow on Overcliff Drive, installed Marie and their two daughters and returned to wherever he happened to be working and having a good old time, visiting them all periodically.

After applying to join a local golf club and finding he was 'blackballed', Louis changed the family name by deed poll from 'Badanski' to 'Brandon'.

When my mother was nineteen, she met my father, and they married at St Catherine's Church, in Southbourne, and promptly moved into a cottage opposite my other grandparents' farm, near Sturminster Marshall. Even though as children we saw so little of 'Grandpa Louis', we always gave him the benefit of the doubt as far as his grandfather skills went ... after all, he always remembered our birthdays, didn't he? Little did we know that the week before each birthday, our mother would write to him to remind him of the date and our individual ages, and we would all in turn be sent a crisp, brown, ten shilling note, which we weren't allowed to spend! Our father insisted on it going in the bank – after all we had our sixpence (now worth 2½p) pocket money every week.

When Marie died, Louis went on to marry his agent, Chris, a lady who looked just like the Duchess of Windsor. They visited us once when I was four, but as they were such strangers, I clearly remember sitting on the stairs refusing to go anywhere near them.

YOUR MOTHER'S HERE!

It's not Chris in the picture below, but it is on the same theme. Paul remembered me sitting on the stairs when Grandpa Louis and Chris came to visit, as you will have seen in the sketch he did, shown earlier on page 30.

LOUIS and ROSE

Chris died a few years later, and Louis married Rose, a lady who he thought owned an establishment selling fur coats. I am not sure at which point he realised that she was not the owner, but was the manageress – probably at the same time she found out that the 'Club' he had half shares in, was not a nightclub, more a gambling den.

When I was nineteen and studying fabric design as my craft at art school, I and two others went up to Manchester for a few days to join a party of students who were being shown around some fabric printing factories.

It was the bad winter of 1963, and we had flown up from Hurn. My two friends, Mary and Malcolm, were going to fly home, but it was thought a good idea that I should catch a train to Leeds to visit 'Grandpa Louis' and Rose.

When I arrived, Rose was a little taken aback at my hippy appearance. She had told her friends, "Louis's granddaughter is visiting us and I will bring her to meet you for coffee," and had arranged to see them in their favourite restaurant. She insisted that I wear one of her coats, rather than my art student uniform of scruffy duffle coat.

After the coffee fiasco, we went to Grandpa Louis's club. It was down in a cellar below street level and the only decorations, as I recall, were a series of blackboards and chalks.

Thanks to my other grandparents, I recognised some of the names on the boards as belonging to racehorses. There was only one concession to comfort in the cellar – a small kitchenette on the side.

Louis's luck as a husband was not good ... Rose died the following year. Unable to look after himself, he advertised for a housekeeper, and on finding her, he installed her and her daughter in his house.

I don't know their names; they didn't stay long enough for my mother to find out, as they did a moonlight flit, taking with them some of his silver and a few other things that took their fancy.

To give him credit, Louis's partner at the club then took responsibility for him and arranged things, enabling him to spend the remainder of his life in a comfortable Jewish care home, although my mother was a trifle surprised to see at his funeral a few gentlemen wearing some of his distinctive jewellery.

On one of his rare visits to Bournemouth towards the end of his life, just before Ted and I were married, Grandpa Louis invited us to join him for dinner in his hotel. Even though it had been many, many years since he had lived in Bournemouth, throughout the meal people were recognising him and coming up to him, appearing so pleased to see him. I wish I had known him better, he must have been quite a character, and I like to think it is his artistic genes that I have inherited. I wonder if he would have liked what I do ...

AUNT ZONA and JACK

Auntie Zona, my mother's elder sister, was beautiful, but intimidating. She was married to Jack Dawson and they lived in an 'upside down' house in Bournemouth. Their bedroom was downstairs, next to the kitchen, and their drawing room was upstairs … quite unusual in the late 1940s. The frontage of the house was that of a terraced Victorian villa, belying what was inside.

Their main interest in life was the theatre and they were on friendly terms with many actors and actresses, some becoming famous, some not.

Charles Gray, who appeared in the James Bond films as a baddie and was always portrayed clutching a cat, was one friend who used to spend a lot of time with them. He also took the part of Mycroft, Sherlock Holmes' elder brother, in the TV series a few years ago. He was a square-shaped person and I always associate pale blue jumpers with him. I remember visiting his mother with my Auntie Zona one afternoon and she complimented me on my neatly smocked dress. Little did she know what a miracle it was to see me neat and tidy at all.

As Auntie Zona was my second godmother, I would occasionally be despatched to spend a few days with her and Uncle Jack. They had no children of their own and weren't quite sure what to do with me. Because their friends were often 'working' in the evenings, Auntie Zona and Uncle Jack would entertain them in the afternoons and I would find myself despatched to my bedroom to rest. At the old age of five, my enforced banishment seemed a waste of time.

Not feeling in the least bit tired one particular afternoon and not finding their selection of books that interesting, as they were mostly on ballet, I decided that the hat with the buzzard's head pinned on the crown, that I had also been given to play with, might be of interest, but on closer examination it struck me as rather repellent, so I put that to one side, climbed out of bed and started rummaging through the dressing table drawers to see what I could find. It was then that I discovered two strange spongy objects, looking like a rubber ball that had been cut in two equal halves. What were they? Putting one on each hand and nudging open the bedroom and lounge doors, I went into the 'salon' to ask.

The room was full of people of all sexes, lounging around, smoking, laughing and drinking, and when I asked in a squeaky, five-year-old voice what these objects were, these people became hysterical with laughter. I couldn't think why … I was deadly serious, I just wanted to know, and when I heard the word 'falsies' I was none the wiser.

When aged six, I was invited to go to the ballet with my Aunt Zona, and there I met another little girl of the same age as me. I had no idea who she was. I can't honestly say I took to her then, as there she stood in a pink party frock with a white angora bolero, and sporting a pair of pretty shoes with dainty socks. I was in an ordinary dress and school shoes.

I later met the 'little girl' when we were in our 30s and found out that her father was my mother's Cousin Leon from Dublin – he of the hair dye incident. Laurie and I have remained in contact ever since and I find her a great support.

In 1952, Auntie Zona and Uncle Jack took the tenancy of 'The Coventry Arms' at Corfe Mullen, just a mile from our farm, turning the pub into a watering hole for theatre buffs and filling the walls with signed, framed photographs of many famous people.

Charles Gray, Zona, Barbara, Gerald, Edna (Gerald's wife) & George

Auntie Zona took up pastel painting, using their assorted cats as models, and she gained quite a reputation, selling her paintings in the pub.

Uncle Jack was very fond of me and when I was in Wimborne Hospital having my appendix out, he would visit daily, as David had a bad throat infection and none of the family were allowed in to see me. Being nine, a year too old for the children's ward, I was put in the women's ward and I found it terrifying. It was mid-November, the time of dark evenings, and I was horribly homesick. To this day when the nights start to draw in I feel very low.

Auntie Zona died, leaving Uncle Jack to run the pub, and then he met and married Jill, 25 years his junior. A new career was embarked on when they left The Coventry, and Uncle Jack concentrated on his other love … antiques, becoming an expert in clocks. Jack and Jill spent their time between France, the antiques and, his first love, the theatre.

At 97 he was widowed for the second time, but insisted he continued to live at home with a live-in carer. He was very proud of the fact that he had never, ever, spent a night in hospital. At 99 he fell, breaking his leg, and the following morning was taken to Dorchester Hospital to be mended. When I phoned to ask how things had gone, the Sister in charge told me sadly, "I am afraid your uncle died in theatre." Jack had a lovely sense of humour and would have appreciated the irony of the situation.

Jack in 2002

The cartoon by 'Gobi', the Swedish illustrator, shows what happens to a gentleman's eyesight when he has partaken of too many cocktails. It was the one thing in Jack's house that I loved from childhood, and it now hangs on our wall as a warning to my family … not that they take much notice.

I sometimes felt a bit out of step with my father's family, even though I loved them dearly and I know they loved me, but Zona, Jack, and in turn Jill, were much more interesting with all their oddities, and treated me as if they knew I had something to say.

AUNTIE RENE

Rene, George and Olive

Closer to me when I was a child, was Auntie Rene, my father's eldest sister, some 21 months his senior and a bit of a 'gal'. I was very attached to her as a small child, as she looked after me a great deal when our mother was ill.

In the months leading up to D-Day, people were encouraged to be welcoming to the American G.Is and to invite them into their homes. Auntie Rene did her bit, and more than one G.I. found himself drinking gallons of tea from Granny's large tea pot on a Sunday afternoon.

I was born in February of that year, so one particular G.I. by the name of Bill Sparrow, was asked to be my godfather and kindly accepted.

Aunt Rene and baby Suzan

In due course, Bill and his comrades left to take part in the Normandy landings and, apart from a couple of photos of Bill, his wife and their small son, taken a few years later, we heard no more. At least, we believe he survived.

Auntie Rene was, in her own right, an accomplished horsewoman and used to help with the showing of Granddad and Olive's ponies. She was proud of having been awarded a trophy by Princess Margaret, standing in for Olive as she was too shy to meet the Princess herself. The trophy was for yet another championship won by Dolly Grey IX.

Olive leads the field in a point to point

Even though Rene was such a good rider, it was a family joke that if ever she was to come off her horse or pony, she would always land on her head.

Suzan, Lizzie and Aunt Rene

Auntie Rene lived at home with her parents, her sister Olive, and her Aunt Ethel, until marrying when she was 38. Then, aged 40 she gave birth on April 1st, six weeks prematurely, to a baby girl, whom we children believed was our one and only cousin, calling her 'Patricia Elizabeth', or 'Lizzie' as we know her.

Years later, we learned that Auntie Rene had previously been engaged to a neighbouring farmer, but when she became pregnant he refused to do the decent thing, and, even though my father was sent to sort him out, he would not stand by her. In the way of things in the 50s, and under the circumstances, she gave in and her son was adopted shortly after his birth.

It broke her heart, and her sister, our Aunt Olive, told me when things came to light many years later, that she used to lie in bed, in the adjoining bedroom to Rene's, listening to her muffled sobs. Her son was adopted, spent a happy childhood in Wales and 'found us all' a few years ago, I am glad to say. He is living now not far away from my 'baby' brother Robin and his family, who live in St Albans.

Auntie Rene, her husband, Uncle Harry, and Lizzie moved to Parkstone when Lizzie was less than a year old, living just a couple of doors away from a family by the name of Gollup. Being an all-girl family, the games the Gollops played were different from the Cowboys and Indians, or hunting type of adventures that I was used to on the farm, and it was from them that I learnt about girlie things, like hopscotch. The aunt living with them was also an aunt of Alec Guinness.

Aunt Rene, with Elizabeth and Suzan on a grey stallion

Lizzie with Dolly Grey IX and foal

I spent many a happy weekend at Auntie Rene's house, and these continued even when I was at art school, which wasn't too far away from where they were living. She was always interested in what I was working on, and encouraged me. When Uncle Harry, a bookmaker, went off to his club in the evening, Auntie Rene allowed me to go into his office and play with one of the old typewriters, having been threatened with dire consequences if I should break it.

In time, Aunt Ethel died, Granddad was ill, Granny ageing, and Olive unable to cope, so Auntie Rene moved back to Brockenhurst to help care for her parents.

It was no secret that Auntie Rene enjoyed a 'tipple' and got herself into some spectacular scrapes, but she was one of the best. My father, George, died at 73 of heart problems, as did his sister, Olive, at the same age, but Auntie Rene, in spite of her little habit, and having been warned by the medical fraternity that she would regret it, went on to be 84.

AUNTIE ETHEL

All my farming and rural paintings contain an element of my father's family. My mother, who they took under their wings when she lost her own mother at the age of 21, used to say it was like 'Cold Comfort Farm'. Paul, David and I loved them all dearly, as odd as they could be.

Ethel, or just 'Auntie' as we all knew her whatever generation we belonged to, was the sister closest to Granny, having lived with Granny and Granddad since their first baby Rene was born. Later on, my father George and then my aunt Olive were born, and it seems Auntie Ethel looked after them all. The fact that she was as deaf as a post, having had measles in her early 20s, could have been a bonus with three unruly farm children, a trait followed by my brothers and I in our turn.

Not only was Auntie deaf thanks to the measles, it had also turned her hair white almost overnight. She then caught another illness from a local dairy, not Granddad's, and it made her refuse to eat or drink anything that contained milk ... a bit of an odd thing, living on a dairy farm. She stuck to her guns and never drank milk again, not even when it came from Primrose, and in consequence lost all her teeth and developed brittle bones.

From the left:
Auntie Nell
Auntie Ethel
and Granny

Auntie's character was that of a quiet, reclusive, naive, shockable and industrious spinster. The one light in her life was my brother Paul.

I often paint my assorted elderly female relatives in a variety of situations; on the farm, indoors, chatting together, but not on the beach. Neither Granny or Ethel spent time sunbathing at the seaside, and if their hair was not already white, it would soon have been ... the thought of being seen in a state of undress would have been dreadful.

Although they knew I was at art school, I don't think any of them realised what a 'Life Class' entailed. Had I told Auntie what took place, I think she would either have swallowed the large handkerchief that she always held to her mouth, or fainted on the spot.

There was one dash of colour in Auntie's life, where, just as Granny and Auntie Nell liked their navy blue, Auntie rather liked her maroon cardigans.

AUNTIE NELL

Auntie Nell was another of Granny and Ethel's sisters. She was very tall and slim, wore thin spectacles and had a 'cottage loaf' bun of fine, white hair. Like Granny, she was nearly always dressed in navy blue.

Auntie Nell never mentioned her husband, and I think she may have been on her own for a long time, running an off license in Southbourne. My granddad's sister, Hilda, did not approve of alcohol, so that must have been fun at family get-togethers!

In later life, Auntie Nell lived with her widowed daughter, Ivy, dividing their house into two separate flats, which was a very successful arrangement. These two tall, thin characters crop up now and again in my paintings, usually in deep conversation.

We had been living at The Stocks Inn for a few years, when Auntie Nell died. After the church service, the family went back to the house that Ivy shared with her mother, where tea and sandwiches were administered in large quantities. A tearful Ivy was sitting with commiserating neighbours, at a table cluttered with all sorts of cups and saucers. Under orders from my father, I was helping to clear the dirty crockery away and taking them into the kitchen to be washed up. I then committed a most awful faux pas by using a pub phrase and saying to Ivy, as I took away her empty cup and saucer, "Is this a dead one?" The silence in the car as we drove home was deafening.

THE CESSPIT INCIDENT

I can't think of our time at Henbury Farm without calling to mind 'the Cesspit Incident', which resulted in my awful fear of water and inability ever to learn to swim. I could easily have drowned that day if it hadn't been for the quick thinking of Ilsie, a German girl who was living with us at the time.

We three children had been warned by our father NOT to go to the small paddock by the side of the house, as the cesspit lid was cracked. Hmm, not the best thing to have told us! David and I went straight out to have a look, and having been joined by our two friends from across the park and found the said lid of no great interest, we decided on yet another game of Cowboys and Indians.

The paddock beside Henbury farmhouse, the location of the cess pit.

I was usually type-cast as the saloon gal, but in this instance I was a cowboy and David my horse. I put the belt from my coat around his waist and we jumped over the lid … well David did, I went straight down into the liquid mess.

Once I had righted myself in this goo, I found it was deeper than I was tall, and I was standing on a narrow ledge.

The boys ran to get help, but our mother, when told I had fallen into a hole in the ground, and thinking that we would not have disobeyed our father, ran off with the protesting boys in hot pursuit … to the slurry pit in the dairy yard.

Ilsie was waiting at the bus stop to go to Wimborne. She heard all the commotion, and guessing that we had ignored what we had been told, came straight to the cesspit, where she leant over the edge and, being a strong girl, was able to reach down and pull me out by my left arm.

As soon as my mother realised that I was safe, she immediately phoned our doctor to ask if there was a chance that I might have picked up some FOUL disease from my experience. His reply was, "Not unless someone with a FOUL disease has used your lavatory."

My indignant mother answered, "How can I telephone people on a Saturday afternoon and ask them a question like that?" and promptly put the phone down.

A hot bath was then decided on, but there was no hot water. So the copper that was normally used for chicken mash was swilled out and filled with cold water, whilst I stood outside the back door dripping and smelling strongly.

The tepid water was finally taken upstairs, where I was ordered to bath and go straight to bed.

… hence my fear of water and drowning.

A few years later, when I was supposed to be learning to swim at school, the instructor said, "You'll never learn in a hundred years."

I am still proving him right.

DO AS YOUR FATHER SAYS

There came a day when our father gave in to our mother's 'nagging' and agreed to start giving my brother, David, and me riding lessons.

Our elder brother, Paul, could already ride quite well. Our father had been a National Hunt jockey, but so far, apart from messing about with ponies and the old Shire horse, we had not been taught to ride properly.

That morning, David was taken down to the village, Sturminster Marshall, and back again, on 'Kit', our little Welsh pony. On their return, I started a fuss, as I wanted my lesson. I wasn't nicknamed 'Foghorn Annie' for nothing … there was just enough time before lunch for a quick lesson, so off we set in the direction of Corfe Mullen, my father on his big horse and me on Kit with a leading rein.

We were just nearing home, when the stallion in a nearby field started to show interest in Kit. She was not impressed and broke into a trot to get away. As traffic was coming from the other way, my father dropped the leading rein, shouting at me, "HANG ON. WHATEVER YOU DO, HANG ON!" I remember thinking, 'Blow that for a game of soldiers,' and taking my feet out of the stirrups. I launched myself off Kit, landing on the nearside grassy bank and dislocating my shoulder.

There was a certain lack of sympathy from my brothers, as I was put in the car and taken off to our doctor for attention, meaning the boys had to wait for their lunch.

Kit trotted home and was fine.

In time I learned to stay on, but I am not an accomplished rider. My poor grandfather, Ted Burry, could never understand how a granddaughter of his was more interested in books and painting, than horses.

KNITTING

In the autumn of 1939, my father had a serious flying accident during training at Hamble, near Southampton. The accident resulted in him cracking his skull, amongst other things, and he was hospitalised for a few months. During his enforced stay, he learnt to knit and became quite accomplished. He was extremely proud of a large, bulky sweater that he created, and he still wore it on the odd occasion years later, although by then it was a bit tattered. In the photo is Ginny, a favourite dog.

When I was seven he taught me the basic skills of knitting and, thanks to him, it is something I have always enjoyed, along with sewing. I loved making dolly clothes and, later on, clothes for our three babies as they arrived ... and then more dolly and teddy clothes.

When my husband, Ted, and I used to take our two small daughters off for a day on the beach, I would dress them in luminous green and pink, hand-knitted jumpers, so that if they wandered off as I sketched or Ted fished, we could see where they were.

On wetter days we all wore bright yellow macs. I cannot understand why they blanche when reminded of how much thought I put into their safety.

Our son Ben was more recently the subject of my colourful and industrious efforts when he was off to a Halloween party.

In reality Ben looks quite 'normal', which this photo of him with his wife, Lucy, shows.

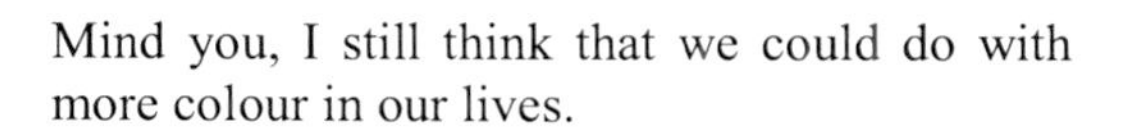

Mind you, I still think that we could do with more colour in our lives.

Now I continue to embarrass my family by wearing my distinctly bright wellies.

GREAT AUNT HILDA and MATRON

Auntie Hilda was my Granddad's sister, some years his junior and closer in every way to their brother, Harold. She was well renowned for her expertise with ponies, at one time running a riding school in Mudeford, where her niece, my Aunt Olive, used to help.

Auntie Hilda never married. According to my father, there was a chap who caught her eye during WW I, but it came to nothing, in fact rumour had it that he was a 'bit of a rotter'. He may have been killed in the war, as so many young men were, no one seemed to know. As far as I am aware that was the end of her romantic dreams and she concentrated on her ponies.

Aunt Hilda showing her New Forest pony

At the time that we children got to know her, Auntie Hilda had moved to a cottage just outside Hartley Wintney, sharing it with her friend, a lady known to all as 'Matron', as she presumably had been in her nursing career.

Matron sported an abundance of red hair, which she pulled back in a bun, saying that it was 'completely natural' and she hadn't 'a single grey hair on her head'. It may have been true, but considering she was well into her late 70s, it was most unlikely.

Matron had a granddaughter, Judy, who was a boarder at Talbot Heath School in Bournemouth, and we children were occasionally invited to spend a few days holiday at the cottage, as we were of a similar age and got on quite well.

Judy seemed to be an expert in things like midnight feasts – a new experience for me, but I doubt that my father would have been impressed if he had found my brothers or me wandering around the kitchen in the middle of the night, especially not after David's earlier little escapade.

My father had a 4.10 shotgun, which he kept high up on brackets above the kitchen door, for the sole purpose of shooting rats on the farm. David came downstairs one night, climbed onto the back of the old armchair where the dogs slept, pulled the gun off the wall, and dropped it, cracking the barrel. Not a popular little boy that day!

During one particular summer holiday, I was the one in trouble. Auntie Hilda suggested I might like to spend a few days with her, probably thinking a break from my brothers would be appreciated before we went back to school. Judy was unable to join us, but no matter, I would be alright on my own. My mother and her friend, Mrs McLellan of Dalmatian fame, were going to a dog show in London, so it was arranged to drop me off at Auntie Hilda's.

I spent a couple of days being the centre of attention, and then I 'blotted my copy book' – to quote my father. Auntie Hilda left me in the field with an old pony of hers, saying she was going to get some shopping and wouldn't be long. She was a bit longer than planned, but appeared at the gate telling me to hurry, we were due at the Red Cross class that she ran every week, and we were going to be late. This class was news to me, but I did as I was told and allowed myself to be bundled into the car and off we went.

Walking across to the hall where the class was to be held, an awful thought must have occurred to Auntie Hilda, as she stopped suddenly and said, "Let me see your hands." They were FILTHY … well, I had been messing about in the field with the pony, no one had told me where we were going, and anyway, when you are an only girl amongst brothers and farm boys, you don't worry about such things as clean hands.

Auntie Hilda was horrified, saying that the first thing she did at the class was to inspect hands and nails for cleanliness, and how could she possibly do that with my 'filthy mitts'? The girls who came to the class couldn't understand why Miss Burry forgot the inspection, she was normally so insistent on such things. If she was still with us today, she would have a fit to see the state of my hands when I have been working hard on a painting.

When painting my groups of ladies, wherever they might be, it is usually a lady like Auntie Hilda who is in charge.

CRICKET

As you may have gathered, sporty things were not my strength. I dreaded the sports lessons at school. All the children that attended Southlands School in Broadstone, Dorset, were expected to play football and cricket, whatever their age or sex, and I didn't take to either, especially when I was knocked off my feet by a well-aimed leather football and winded – I was five at the time. The thought of bats and balls did not appeal at all.

Sports Day was a nightmare too, apart from the day that my father and our form mistress were paired off in the three-legged race.

There was a deep ditch at the bottom of the playing field, just behind the football net, and their brakes failed to work …

Why is it the only thing I remember about that day?

When we all moved to The Stocks Inn, Furzehill, Wimborne, I changed schools and began at Melverley School for Girls.

The following summer it was decided that the older girls should play cricket. No one seemed to know the rules, but as they thought I'd played it before, they assumed I could tell them. To be honest I had never taken much interest and couldn't be sure I knew what I was talking about – nor could they! I found myself dismissed as useless and the last to be chosen for a team. I didn't mind really as I was already well on my way to becoming the class clown.

As the only girl with two brothers I served my 'survival apprenticeship' young, and they had to put up with me as the only sister they had. Paul remembers me winding up David one afternoon when our parents were looking at a cottage near The True Lovers Knot pub, near Blandford, and had gone into the cottage taking Paul with them.

David and I were left in the car, which was parked on a steep incline, and told to 'behave' – no point really saying that to a five and six year old. We can only have been left for a few minutes, when I began to panic in case the brakes failed and the car rolled down the hill. I remember thinking, 'It's no good me shouting for them to come out, but if David was to cry they'll come straight away.' So I frightened David, by saying I was afraid of the car rolling down the hill. He started to yell loudly and out they came … and then it was my turn to yell at what I considered an unfair telling off.

Oh, happy days! I still feel ashamed of being so devious.

HOCKEY

Winter meant 'hockey' and I didn't like it – all those painful bangs on the ankles, blue knees, and the long, cold walk across the town to the playing field.

I'd had TB as a small child and one winter, when I seemed to have one cold after another, I was excused this Thursday afternoon torture and, as I was 'an obedient child'(!) I was allowed to stay in my classroom on my own, having been given extra History or English essays.

I didn't see it as a punishment, but I wasn't allowed to spend the afternoon painting – that was a punishment!

To be left alone to draw and paint was my idea of heaven … a point I often had to make to my noisy, lively brothers.

I must have complained a lot, and Paul obviously remembered.

He drew me this lovely cartoon in the book he made for my birthday (the one with the big '0' in it).

It's entitled 'THE ARTIST'.

CATS

My grandmother had many cats on the farm, but only one came indoors – Blackie – and that was for her daily inspection for fleas or ticks, carried out by my father's sister, Olive, when she had her habitual ten minute sit-down after lunch, before going out to see to the animals.

My mother's sister, Zona, and her husband, Jack Dawson, kept The Coventry Arms at Corfe Mullen for over twenty-five years. It was a watering hole for artists, actors and 'others'.

Zona and Jack absolutely loved cats. They had three – Todd, a huge, round, black tom, Dora, his 'wife', who appears in the painting below, and one of their offspring, called 'Pig'.

Pig was a big, completely black cat, but he was not what is called 'the full ticket'. He would climb up on a bar stool, fall asleep and suddenly fall off. Somehow he always landed on his feet.

Pig was not adverse to drinking from the copper drip trays that hung under the beer barrels. Sober or not, he was an excellent mouser.

In due course, Maud, a Siamese, and Archibald, a Burmese, added themselves to the household, and considering themselves far superior to Todd, Dora and Pig, kept their distance, insisting on sleeping in the airing cupboard. There was always a faint whiff of cat about my aunt and uncle.

SANDY

I often include cats in my paintings – not the 'ahhh' kind though, more the curious ones – the observers, just waiting for something to happen. As children we were surrounded by farm cats, dogs, rabbits, horses and all the usual farmyard animals. When I first became aware of Sandy, he was a full grown cat. Apparently, after a visit to the vets at six months old he had never been heard to 'miaow' again. He was struck dumb by whatever happened to him – not altogether surprising. I cannot remember him ever climbing on a knee to be petted, but he was a faithful cat, as we moved him five times during his lifetime of eighteen years and he never went missing.

His one good friend was Gertie, our old Boxer dog, and they would lie together in front of a roaring fire, warming their old bones.

Sandy had a favourite trick that he played on us children. He would curl up on the third stair from the bottom of the staircase and pretend to be fast asleep. We children knew what he was capable of so we used to creep slowly past him.

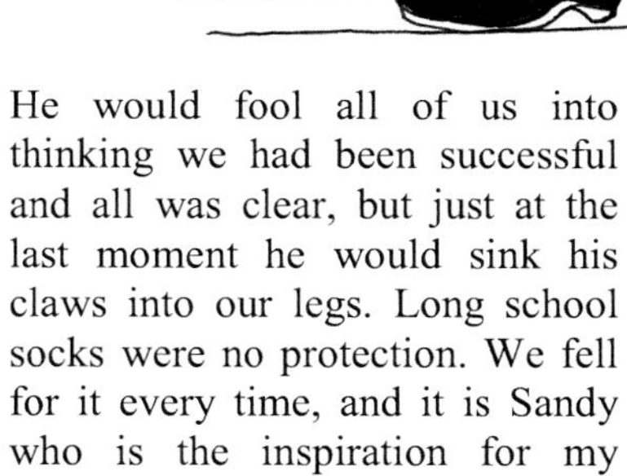

He would fool all of us into thinking we had been successful and all was clear, but just at the last moment he would sink his claws into our legs. Long school socks were no protection. We fell for it every time, and it is Sandy who is the inspiration for my manic cat paintings.

Sandy's reign of terror was also inflicted on all the family dogs, apart from Gertie, and on any unfortunate visiting canine.

BOOZER

Cats appear in all shapes, sizes and colours in my paintings. I have already mentioned Sandy, but when we moved to The Stocks Inn, near Wimborne, in 1955, my father thought a second cat would be a good idea to keep an eye on the mouse population. We had outbuildings, a stable and pig sties at the pub in those days, all gone now, sacrificed to 'the god of car parks'.

I am not sure where Boozer came from, but he quickly became a part of the family, growing into a large ball of black and white fur, with tremendous whiskers.

When still young he survived a savage attack by a couple of dogs belonging to one of our pub characters, a Mr Bill Isaacs (see page 24). Boozer disappeared and then returned to us a few days later, somewhat lighter, but much wiser.

I arrived home from school one day to be met by my bemused mother. "Did you know Boozer can fly?" my mother asked.

I was aware that my mother had been out with her friends that day, so I didn't take much notice.

"No," my mother insisted, "I was coming through the gate and he flew past me."

When I asked my father what all this was about, he explained that he had made a crab sandwich for a customer, closed the fridge and returned to the bar.

Another round of sandwiches was ordered, so he returned to the kitchen and opened the fridge to discover Boozer crouched in the corner just finishing the remains of the crab meat.

In those days my father was athletic – he could have been a shot putter.

Our comments of, "How fortunate that you opened the fridge when you did. Boozer could have suffocated," were ignored.

Boozer and Sandy only tolerated each other. I don't think they exchanged more than a civil nod, and after the flying incident Boozer ignored my father.

Boozer was actually a black and white cat. I have taken artist's license in painting him all black and madly fluffy in the picture above.

GRANNY AND HER FOWLS

Granny loved cats and they knew this, hopping onto her lap as soon as she sat down. She also always kept chickens, supplying most of Balmer Lawn Road with fresh eggs. She may not have been involved with the bigger animals on the farm, but she enjoyed looking after the henhouse full of her feathered friends.

I loved spending time with Granny, and as a treat I was allowed to help her collect eggs. I thought it was wonderful to put my hands into the laying boxes and retrieve a still warm egg from under a soft, fluffy bottomed hen, often much to their indignation.

Chickens are amazingly tough and so long as they have somewhere safe, dry and out of the wind as soon as it is getting dark, they will be fine.

But cats and dogs, just like us humans, like nothing better than being indoors with a cosy fire when it's cold outside.

SNOW

It has been snowing and the farmer and his wife are attending to the old horse and the chickens. The farmer's wife is sporting a pair of what were known as 'moon boots'. I had a blue pair just like hers and was very proud of them, but they were absolutely useless in cold snowy weather, in fact they were lethal.

Living in the depths of Wiltshire, you could bet you life that if there was any snow forecast we would get it, and in the painting below it has been snowing once more. No one can go to work … or school. The children are making the most of an extra day off school. and so are the young lovers, standing whispering sweet nothings to each other and making themselves prime targets for the mischievous 'truants'. Appearing to be busy with building a snowman, the children are just waiting for their chance to throw a snowball at the couple. The toddler is trying to decide whether to believe his brother and sisters when they say the snow tastes like ice cream.

This painting is of a stable yard covered in a light dusting of snow, where the small boy is offering an apple to a stabled horse. The other child is a little nervous, much as we were as children, having been warned that Granddad's stallion, Blunderbuss, could not always be trusted.
We were told to keep away from him.

The first thing you learn on a farm is that whatever the weather, or however you are feeling, the animals must be fed and looked after properly before you think about yourself.

CHRISTMAS

Christmas was always something that we, as most children, looked forward to, but it never seemed to go as planned. I often paint this subject and the chaos that goes with it, it is one of those themes with so many possibilities.

The first Christmas that I was aware of was the one when my eldest brother Paul and I were recovering from measles. Paul had not long been at school and had contracted measles, bringing it home.

Come Christmas and our brother, David, was still very poorly.

On Christmas day Paul and I were taken by our father on a brief visit to our grandparents. It was dark when we returned home and we let ourselves into the house under strict instructions not to make too much noise in case David was sleeping …

… he wasn't. As we crept up the stairs I could hear David's plaintive, tired crying, sounding all the sadder as David was a tough little boy who rarely cried. He was sitting in a chair being nursed by our mother, by the fire in a hot, stuffy bedroom.

After all these long, long years, the sound of his crying is still a poignant memory.

Another Christmas a few years later, we were settling down by the fire on Christmas Eve when there was a knock on the front door. Our mother tipped the dog off her lap and went to answer it. On opening the door she said in a loud voice, "Oh I say, it's Father Christmas! Oh do come in." And in he came, a tall figure dressed in an ill-fitting red costume, wearing black wellingtons covered in farmyard muck, sporting a suspect white beard, and carrying a limp sack on his back. 'Hmm,' I thought to myself, 'he looks a lot like Adrian (a man who worked on the farm). I had better go along with it or I might spoil any chance of a present.' It proved a wise decision.

The following year as Christmas approached, my brother David 'discovered' our Christmas presents in our parents' wardrobe … a pure accident of course. He informed me that I was to be given an Archie Andrews ventriloquist doll, dressed in grey flannels and a navy blue blazer. I was more than a little surprised, as to my knowledge I had never ever expressed any desire to be a ventriloquist. I just hoped David had made a mistake … he hadn't!

My Aunt Olive, whose life revolved around ponies, the farm and the garden, made up for the 'doll'. She had very thoughtfully given me an adult's set of beautiful Winsor and Newton watercolours in a shiny black box. Even though I was only eight, I knew they were special, and for days could not bear to be parted from them. Woe betide anyone who went near them.

As an artist I am forever buying brushes, paints, paper and canvases, but nothing compares with the way I felt on receiving those wonderful watercolours. I wasn't completely ungrateful for the dummy though and he was played with, but I think he met an untimely end at the jaws of one of our numerous dogs.

This painting is of families queuing up to meet 'Santa'. The children are over-excited and crying, and the parents impatient. A pregnant mother is wondering what on earth she has let herself in for. The idea for the painting came from a visit my husband, Ted, and I made with our small daughters to see Santa one Saturday morning not long before Christmas. The Southampton store was very busy, the queue was long and the girls' tempers short. When we finally made it into Santa's Grotto, there were two Santas, sitting side by side. Both girls were given a present and didn't find the situation strange at all, in fact it saved a heated sibling argument about who was going to chat to Santa first!

MRS BAGSHOTT

This lady was an unlikely friend of our mother. Where she came from, or how our mother knew her, remains a mystery to this day. Maybe they met when helping our Auntie Zona and her husband at their pub, The Coventry Arms. Neither I, nor my brothers, ever knew her Christian name, and we would never have presumed to call her anything other than 'Mrs Bagshott'.

When we moved to The Stocks Inn she seemed to disappear, although she did help with the actual move. The one thing I can remember about her was her ENORMOUS bosom, it was extraordinary, and being very short she looked rather odd, having the appearance of a plump pigeon. According to our mother this large bosom was controlled by specially made brassieres.

Over the weekend when we moved from the farm to the pub, I was dispatched to stay with yet another family friend, to keep me out of the way. This lady was Pat McLellan, well known for breeding champion Dalmatians.

On my arrival at our new home, I found that I was expected to share my 'new' bedroom with Mrs Bagshott for a couple of nights, until she went home.

I can't honestly say I was happy about it, and I think Mrs Bagshott would rather not have had a nosey eleven-year-old looking at her with curiosity, intrigued by her voluminous, long sleeved, high necked, down to the ground, nightgown, under which it was obvious she was still wearing the aforementioned 'armour plated' garment.

I often portray ladies of Mrs Bagshott's ilk in my paintings – larger than life, slightly disapproving but always in charge.

Going back to my mother's friend, Pat McLellan – she had a most beautiful champion Dalmatian bitch, 'Wendy' by name.

Wendy was entered for Crufts in the forthcoming year, and having produced an unusually large litter of puppies, it was felt there were too many for her to feed and be ready to appear at the show.

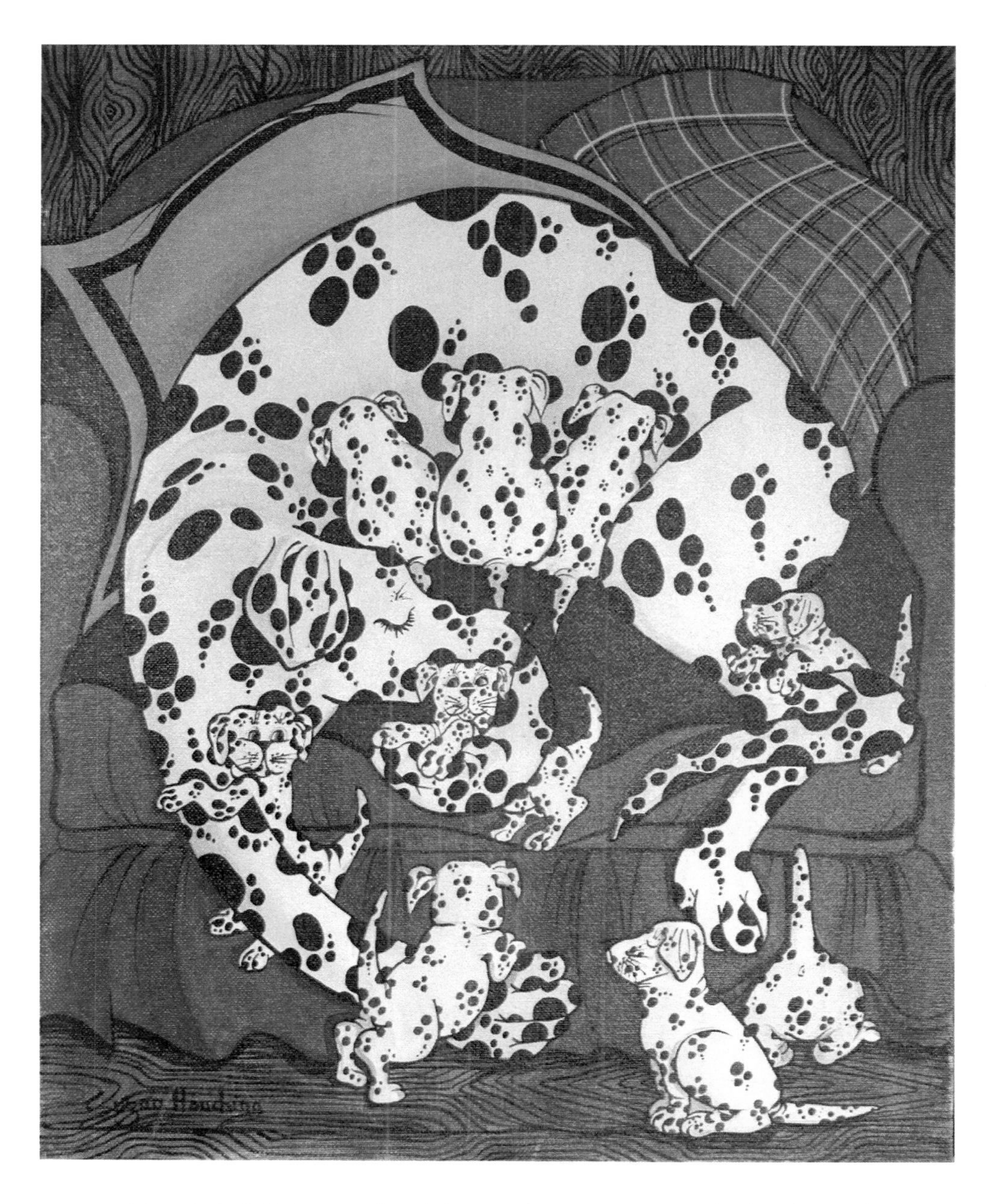

After their initial start, six of the puppies came to us to be hand reared under the care of my mother. We children were allowed to help with the bottle feeding, which I thoroughly enjoyed. The six puppies all did very well and, along with all their brothers and sisters, grew into beautiful dogs – all chips off the old block.

I have always been fascinated by Dalmatians, each one with their own distinctive pattern of spots, black or brown, on white.

THE DOG SHOW

A Mrs Bagshott lookalike shows up here at the dog show. She is showing a chunky-looking Boxer dog, coloured like my father's favourite dog 'Gertie'.

Our Dachshund dog, Percy, who you can see on the following page, was bred for showing, but it was not to be – probably lucky for him, because he preferred chasing the pigs on the farm.

PERCY and GERTIE

I have the greatest respect for animals, and having been surrounded by them most of my life, I am under no illusions as to what they are capable of or the things they can get up to. My mother had a favourite Dachshund bitch called 'Ping', who in due course gave birth to a litter of six puppies. We children were a little afraid of Ping, as she was known to bite occasionally. My mother decided to keep one of the puppies, but her first choice showed signs of taking after his mother, so 'Percy' was settled on.

Percy looked as if he would grow into a handsome dog destined for the show ring, but after scarring his left flank that was out of the question. His next career move was to be a stud dog, but he showed no aptitude for that whatsoever, so he spent his long life lounging around and pretending, with his deep Dachshund bark, that he was a guard dog. He was a lovely dog and appears often in my paintings.

To keep him company when we moved to The Stocks Inn, 'Noni', a gentle natured Dalmatian, became part of the family, and she too is represented in my work. Sadly we lost Noni when she developed a bone disease and had to be put down. We children were heartbroken … and then 'Gertie', a Boxer puppy, joined us.

Of all the dogs I have ever known, Gertie was the one with the greatest character. She took to the pub life and drink quite easily, occasionally accepting a glass of egg flip from a customer. She would take her drink (just the one) from a long liqueur glass, and then stagger away to sleep it off by the fire with Percy, or if he was in a good mood, with Sandy the cat.

CINDY

In the days when I was a child, pubs were closed for the afternoon … no such thing as all day opening.

My father liked his afternoon walks with the dogs, usually leaving before we children came home from school.

In the summer, being a bit of a sun worshiper, he would close the pub, smother himself with olive oil, put on his knitted maroon woollen bathing trunks, made by his own fair hands, and his old wellington boots and sun glasses, and set off across the fields to call on our barman and his wife.

They lived in a small thatched cottage in the village, and with them, amongst all the brass, china, paintings, and cases of spiders, butterflies and the odd creepy crawly, lived Cindy, their pampered pooch.

Cindy was a very pretty mongrel, covered in long curly hair, sporting a 'top knot' tied up in a bow, and smelling of perfume.

Percy and Gertie were no fools and they knew full well that out in the kitchen would be a dish of 'something special' for Cindy's tea.

One dog would attract her attention and the other would sneak out into the kitchen and eat the tasty treats. Poor Cindy, she never learnt, but she does feature in my paintings at times.

ROSA and the RASPBERRIES

Animals can be rather embarrassing at times. One cold Saturday morning, a local chicken farmer called at the farmhouse to speak to my father. The farmer was a tall, lean man, dressed in a shiny black suit and boots, and he moved in a jumpy way, just like a chicken.

He was invited in and joined my mother by the roaring fire, sitting in the opposite bulky armchair from her. This man was also a strict, sober, lay preacher and sadly he had no sense of humour at all.

We children were listening to *Children's Favourites* on the wireless and making a lot of noise, so we were asked to go and play elsewhere. Had we stayed we would have made matters worse I am sure.

My mortified mother told us later what had happened …

Apparently, every so often there was the sound of a loud raspberry … from my mother's direction. The farmer looked at her in horror, but was too polite to make any comment. What he did not know was that curled up behind our mother in the big chair, out of sight to him, was yet another of our flatulent dogs, 'Rosa' by name … a little unsuitable!

GERMAN SHEPHERDS

Jessie

There have been five German Shepherd dogs in our family over the years. All have been slightly eccentric, but wonderfully faithful. If I want a strong dog that commands respect, I will paint a German Shepherd.

'Major' was the first and he belonged to my mother as a child. Next came 'Bella' who belonged to my father-in-law when he retired from the sea.

When Ted and I moved to The Swordsman, we soon realised that a dog was needed. We heard about a litter of puppies and contacted the breeders. It was arranged for Ted to drive down to Wool, near Corfe Castle, to collect our puppy. She was just ten weeks old, and by the time they returned home 'Jessie', as we came to call her, and Ted had bonded. She was always Ted's dog.

Unlike a lot of dogs, Jessie never barked indoors, apart from a single occasion, when having seen the last customer off the premises one night, Ted was about to lock the door and it was re-opened by one of our darts players, who had come back having forgotten his coat. Jessie gave one almighty 'WOOF', nearly scaring the man out of his wits.

Jessie was wonderful with children, so much so that customers could safely leave their youngsters with ours in the garden, knowing Jessie would be looking out for them. No one, not even their parents, could remove a child unless Ted or I went out to say it was alright.

When Ben was born, he would be asleep in his pram in the small living room off the bar and at the first sign of his stirring Jessie would alert me. At the bottom of our large wilderness of a garden was farmland, and as a tiny boy our son Ben could be found leaning on the fence, watched by Jessie, and singing nursery rhymes to the dairy cows as they munched happily on the grass.

Sadly, we lost Jessie at the age of seven, and it broke Ted's heart.

Josie

Having lost Jessie, we debated at great length about another dog and decide to wait a while. We held out for four days and then we were told by one of our customers about a litter of German Shepherd puppies born in a pub in Salisbury. It sounded ideal, the puppy would be used to the noise, smell and general goings on of pub life. Our daughter Kait begged her father to take her to see them. Off they went and returned two hours later with a bedraggled, car sick bundle of fur. She came across to me, sat on my feet, and became MY dog from that moment, and the girls gave her the name 'Josie'.

The problem with her soon showed itself – she had inherited from her mother a dislike of men.

Luckily, Josie was alright with Ted and other family members and when she was four we moved from our pub, with its large wild garden, to the Burley Club, where we lived in the steward's flat. As we drove away from The Swordsman, our old customers were all frantically waving out of the window, wanting us to stop, which we did, only to realise we had forgotten to put Josie in the car.

As soon as we moved in, Josie chose to sleep by the front door, just in case we decided to move again without telling her. We didn't take her down to the bars as she had never grown out of her bad habit of biting the rear of any man who turned their back on her. All went well, except one particular morning when a young policeman knocked at the flat door, which stood at the top of a flight of stairs. He was looking for the Burley Golf Club, not the Burley Club, and after I gave him directions he turned to go down the steps. Josie saw her chance and bit the seat of his trousers. Fortunately, he quite understood, and continued on his way!

Annie

Years went by and the children all grew up and left home. Kait was living in Portsmouth when she heard about a German Shepherd that was for sale. It was the one thing she longed for, a dog of her own. She visited the house to meet the dog, fell in love with her, but was disappointed when the owner advised her to think again, as she would be out working a lot of the time. A few days later the owner phoned Kait to say she could have her.

Annie was like most of her breed, a one person dog, and she became Kait's shadow. The two of them went through a lot of ups and downs, and as time went by they moved home to live with us.

Even though Annie had a reputation of not really liking small children, she proved us all wrong in a big way. Every Tuesday, before he started full-time school, we used to look after Joe, our daughter Sophie's youngest, and Annie became his devoted slave.

Annie was everything to Kait, but sadly she aged and suffered a severe stroke when she and Kait were out on a walk. On getting her home, the vet was called, but there was nothing to be done other than 'to send her on her way' and then a strange thing happened. As Kait opened the front door minutes after Annie died, there, sitting on the doorstep was a plump hedgehog, it looked up at us for a few moments, turned round and walked away. It made us feel that it had come to collect Annie and take her to where all animals go when they die.

MRS TAYLOR

Mrs Taylor, Suzan and George, with Gertie, Tilley and Tilley's puppies

Mrs Taylor was a treasure, who lived just down the road from our pub, at Furzehill. She proved herself invaluable, especially to my mother who enjoyed her role as 'mine hostess' to the full, so Mrs Taylor took on many of the household tasks for her. Mrs Taylor was a dyed-in-the-wool country woman, rather stout, with a wide, smiling face.

We were a rather disorganised family to say the least, but Mrs Taylor made sure that domestically the house ran relatively smoothly.

She despaired of me as a lazy, stroppy teenager (yes, don't believe the angelic pose in the photo) and of our household of cats, dogs, and the odd hibernating tortoise. Why Percy, our Dachshund, was allowed to sleep under eiderdowns was beyond her, she herself would never have allowed such a thing in her tidy, neat home.

During my first year at Art School I studied dress design, changing to fabric design and printing for the following three years. We concentrated on our 'craft' subject one day a week and the rest of the week was made up with life classes, plant drawing, composition and painting, all with great encouragement on using our sketch books.

Thanks to my first year of dress design, there were times when I felt inspired to create some 'exclusive garment'. Most of them were pretty grim. As I was getting off the college bus one day in Wimborne, I was spotted by my mother who was out shopping, and she quite understandably crossed the road pretending she hadn't seen me, I looked so awful. My mother always looked smart, with her clothes, hair and make-up just so – I didn't. Mrs Taylor was my 'partner in crime' when it came to making my creations, allowing me to use her old sewing machine. She certainly had a sense of humour – my mother and I made her laugh and tear her hair out, making her glad she only had one child – a son.

We children always called her 'Mrs Taylor'. I think her name was Madge, but we would never have dared call her that.

THE PIED PIPER

As a small child I attended Southlands School, in Broadstone, Dorset … long gone now, but a wonderful school, keen on art, music and drama. I loved every minute of my time there.

I think I can remember the names of all my classmates from my early years at school … or nearly all. Oh for that young brain again!

From the left top row: Alec Yarrow, Janet Morris, Heather Milne, Kathleen .... and Bruce Miller. Middle row: Margaret Forrest, Fiona Mallett, Jane Viader, Diana Jarmain and Judith .... Bottom row: Peter Norman, Susan Burry (Suzan) and Fiona McFarlen.

For some reason my great friend Elizabeth Conder is not in the photo. She and I were in the kindergarten together, as was David, and we are friends to this day.

One year at school we put on a performance of *The Pied Piper*.

In the photo I am a villager (third from left) and to my left are Alec Yarrow, Peter Craven and Fiona Mallett. To my right is Margaret Forrest, but the name of the boy I cannot remember. *(Please, dear reader, if you can fill in the gaps in the names, do let me know.)*

The following year I took part in our school's production of *Macbeth*.

Dressed in my mother's cut down 'little black dress', rather plump and grinning with acute embarrassment, I appeared as 'The Third Witch'. I decided there and then that the stage was not for me, I would rather paint the scenery.

Over the years we've lived in Burley I've been involved with the Burley Players … not on stage, but behind the scenes with my paints and brushes, designing the scenery for their plays and pantomimes.

Only then did I realise that if you overpaint a door until it sticks, or if you set the scenery crooked, your hero will be guaranteed to make spectacularly hilarious entries … whether on purpose or not!

SET PAINTING

I love going to the theatre and am always as interested in the scenery as in the performance, be it a play, a musical, a ballet, opera, pantomime or any other show.

Along with a summer production, our local 'Burley Players' put on a pantomime every January, and for the last twenty years my friend, Paul Kew, has painted the scenery. Four backdrops are usually needed, plus two side flaps for each set, and as it is quite a task for one person, ten years ago I also became involved with the scenery painting.

Paul and I sit down once we have seen the script and decide who is going to do what. We take on two backdrops each, but we don't paint together as our styles are vastly different; Paul likes to paint palaces and creepy woods, dungeons and caves, whereas I like to paint the village or town centres, the cottages, their interiors, harbours and boats, which isn't altogether surprising.

Most of my 'normal' paintings are very time consuming and complex, full of all sorts of details, so it's good fun to go down to the village hall with my battered trolley of paints, large brushes, sandwiches and tea. Instead of a canvas, I am faced with a vast blank backdrop and am able to just 'go for it'.

Four years ago our youngest granddaughter, Georgi, was asked to be 'Mary' in the Christingle service in our village church.

Although my needlework is suspect, I applied my years of experience in making costumes for the children and grandchildren, and stitched together Mary's clothes. I even found a Clint Eastwood-style poncho for 'Joseph' who was to be played by Jack Gray, a classmate of Georgi's.

All that was needed was a life-like baby doll, which was kindly supplied by Pat Moore, a lady who lived in Burley, whose hobby was collecting and dressing dolls. The doll she gave me was very convincing, looking just like a new born baby, down to the very last detail, and although 'he' had only one arm, he looked lovely wrapped in a shawl and carried by his 'parents' at the start of the service.

The baby doll then spent the next three years 'resting' ... until last year's pantomime. One of the first scenes of *Sleeping Beauty* was to be the portrayal of the King and Queen with their little new born princess. A 'baby' with suitable costume was needed. I looked in the dressing up chest and found the christening robes that our eldest granddaughter Robyn had worn 23 years before in 1992. It was a rather luxurious affair of lace and satin smock with matching bloomers. I topped it with a lacy bonnet that our son had worn at his christening and the doll went off to his audition.

On the day of the pantomime I held my breath as 'he' was lifted out of his cradle, the one that my husband, Ted, made for our eldest daughter Kait when she was born. Luckily they had heeded my earlier warning, 'please ensure that the Princess Sleeping Beauty's bloomers don't fall off'. An accident in that department would have put a totally different slant on the whole performance, with more than a few gasps of shock from those watching, if not a need for the defibrillator that hangs on the wall outside the village hall, or at least for smelling salts!

As with the stage sets, my village paintings are not true portrayals of real places, but I use my sketches as inspiration. The picture below is of a soft Devon village, based loosely on a sketch I made some years ago of Beer. It is a breezy morning and the wind-blown washing is the main feature.

The painting to the right sprang from sketches I did on holiday in Yorkshire with my friends, Rosemary and John Grant. On Sunday they went golfing, and I spent the day exploring Askrigg village and sketching. The village was used many years ago in filming *All Creatures Great and Small,* and it is full of interesting old grey buildings – a contrast to the warm colours of Beer. The road runs downhill, sharply turning a corner, making the perspective quite challenging. Again there are few people about, apart from two gossiping women and a mother and child – are they the subject of the gossipers ?

INSPIRATIONAL

The fact that Southlands School, my first school, concentrated on music, the arts, and literature, sport, as I remember being of secondary importance, suited me well … so I thought.

I was in the kindergarten class when I experienced my first rejection of a painting. My painting was of 'swans on a lake', I daresay a popular subject for a five-year-old, and I proudly presented it to Madame Page, our French mistress, as a gift. At the end of term, when clearing her desk, she gave it back to me. A painful lesson in artistic rejection learned early in life!

'The Last Of England' by Ford Maddox Brown

My maternal grandfather, Louis Earle Brandon, had two large volumes of art books, both printed in 1901.

One book contained what were considered in Victorian eyes to be the 'One Hundred Best Paintings', all of which were printed in sepia monochrome.

The second book, also all in sepia, was of Victorian nudes. The figures were relatively modest and portrayed in idealistic, classic Grecian statue type poses, but nonetheless considered unsuitable for the eyes of us 'Philistine' children.

I often used to leaf through the 'One Hundred Best Paintings' and I was always drawn, irresistibly, to Ford Maddox Brown's 'The Last Of England'.

A young couple are looking straight out of the painting at the England they are leaving behind, hoping to find a better life elsewhere for themselves and their children, one a small baby tucked well away under his mother's cloak.

Even as a young child I found the painting haunting. The circular composition is unusual and the full colour when I saw it again years later, lived up to expectations.

A friend from our Swordsman days gave me a small copy of the painting, and it hangs on our landing, where I still stop and look at it as I go by.

A CHANCE IN A MILLION

This painting of mine is along similar lines to 'The Last of England'. It shows a young family, all packed up and ready to embark on their ship, the RMS Titanic, but before they leave they are saying their farewells to their family.

The aged parents are troubled and sad at their departure, but, as the young man says, "It's a chance in a million, mother."

How right he was proved to be! I remember our headmistress, Mrs Barnard, reading a graphic account to our class about the sinking of the *Titanic*, on what could have been the 40th anniversary of the disaster, and it gave me nightmares for months.

I think it might have reinforced my fear of water and boats.

Mind you, the same Mrs Barnard used to read us stories about the Spartans and how tough they were, what with babies left on hillsides and boys being taken away from their families at a young age.

Hmm? ... being the sort of child I was, did I think that maybe my brothers might benefit from that sort of treatment?

LIFE CLASS

It was in the late 1950s that my parents took the tenancy of The Stocks Inn, near Wimborne, and we were there for many years. During this time, I finished school and enrolled as a full time student at the Poole College of Art.

My four years at art college proved to be a great eye opener for someone straight from a small, all-girls school.

My father used to display advertising posters for the Pavilion Theatre in Bournemouth, putting them in the pub porch, and he would often be given complimentary tickets. My parents could rarely take the same evening off, so at times he would collect me from college and we would go to see a show.

We set off one evening, full of excitement, with our tickets for the ballet.

One of our 'life' models at college was a lady of rather large proportions. During class one day she told us she was in the 'Corps de Ballet' in the production of *Swan Lake* that was being performed that week in the Pavilion.

No one took her seriously, but coincidently on the day that my father and I were going to the ballet, we settled in our seats, and there she was – as large as life.

At one point she bounced across the stage, and the diminutive male dancer, who caught her, must have been made of strong stuff – all that was noticeable being a slight buckling of the knees and a little staggering.

We had a variety of models over the years, of all shapes, sizes and sexes.

The painting on the next page is a fictitious life class, where the men are painting the model as they would like her to be, and the women in not quite so flattering a way – but funnily enough, more like themselves.

REMEMBERING...

In this picture the elderly couple are looking at a painting executed many years previously by a fellow artist when all of them were young and carefree. It helped their friend, and it helped them to pay their rent when they agreed to model for him.

Are they remembering how handsome and hopeful they were in those far off days, before life and gravity took its toll?

THE PREVIEW

This painting was inspired by an exhibit at the Tate, a sculpture that was short listed for the Turner Prize a few years ago. I won't describe what it depicted, it might put you off your tea, but the work itself was attracting a lot of attention. It didn't win!

In the picture below, the people portray the various reactions that you get at the preview of any art group or society exhibition, no particular one, on its opening night.

The gathered guests are all looking at something … and quite a few are 'not sure what'.

When you are at one of these functions and surrounded by people, it is best never, ever, to pass a comment, good or bad. If you do, you can bet your life the artist, or a friend of the artist, is standing right behind you, listening to every word.

THE PORTRAIT ARTIST

A lady is sitting, having her portrait painted. For diplomacy's sake and to help his bank balance, the artist is painting her as he thinks she would like to be portrayed, rather than as she is in reality. The work is taking place in the artist's studio, which is full of other pictures and paints. The faithful dog is watching and the cats are waiting their moment to wreak havoc.

My maternal grandfather, Louis Earle Brandon (Badanski) made a name for himself as a portrait painter, specialising in miniatures. His father before him, Simeon, had been an active political protestor in his younger days, according to my mother. Maybe that explains why I used to go on protest meetings and wave banners.

Many years ago when we lived in Dinton, our village school was threatened with closure, but after banding together, painting banners and slogans on shirts (that was my job), hiring a coach and attending various council meetings etc. we managed to save the school, much to the delight and relief of the village.

Over 30 years later the school is still going strong, and very much a part of the village. The children and parents who fought for the school all those years ago, have gone their separate ways, but it was a great victory for us all. I still have my shirt in the dressing up box, but if I tried to put it on, I would find it a bit too snug.

THE HOUCHING IN-LAWS

Kathleen Rosamund Lyle Gingell, or 'Kit' as she was known.

My mother-in-law, Kit, and father-in-law, Arthur, were lovely people and more than just in-laws to me. Kit couldn't read a note of music, even though her mother was a music teacher. Even so, she was an accomplished pianist, and in 1914, at the age of fourteen, she applied for a job at the Woolston Picture House, to play for the silent movies. The programme changed twice a week and Kit would compose new music for every film.

As a young girl she had dreamt of going on the stage, but her father would not allow it, and playing for the films was the next best thing, making her feel part of the entertainment world. Her music was extraordinary, and she was still composing music decades later, being very proud of her Bluthner grand piano. She loved her job and only gave it up when the talkies came in the early 1920s.

By this time Kit had met Arthur Cecil Houching, and they married on April 26th 1923, at the same time and on the same day as the Duke and Duchess of York, later to be King George VI and Lady Elizabeth Bowes-Lyon the Queen Mother. Kit and Arthur were married at Holy Rood Church, in Southampton, the church that was bombed in World War II and whose ruins became a memorial to the Merchant Navy and to the RMS Titanic.

Arthur was away nearly all the time, being in the Merchant Navy, sailing out of Liverpool. When Helen and Ted were born, Kit would have found life hard bringing up two children virtually on her own, had it not been for the help of her parents.

Kit, Arthur, 'Auntie' Inez (Kit's sister) and Suzan

Apart from her children, the one thing Kit loved was collecting antiques and curios. She soon outgrew their house and bought a thatched cottage to match her collection. She loved going out to tea and knew every tearoom and antique shop for miles around.

After living on her own when Arthur died, she moved to live opposite us at The Swordsman, and was a great help to me with the children. Sophie would go across to her flat on a Saturday morning and chat to 'Grandma' for hours about her adventures in the war, hearing how she coped, losing two homes in the bombing, and about her daughter Helen's four marriages, a subject Sophie found fascinating. At nearly 80 years old, Grandma was still playing 'garages' with Ben. None of the children could put a foot wrong in her eyes. I often paint kind grannies surrounded by an assortment of toys and grandchildren, or chatting over a cup of tea with a friend in a café.

Arthur Cecil Houching

Arthur was born in Tooting, London, and when it was found he was suffering from TB, his doctor told his parents that the only hope was to get him out of London and send him to sea.

Aged fourteen, he found himself in the Cunard White Star Company at the beginning of a long career in the Merchant Navy. Apart from World Wars I and II, in which he served in the Royal Navy, Arthur spent his whole working life with Cunard, retiring as Restaurant Manager on the *Queen Mary*.

Arthur on HMS Activity Iceland, May 1943

On the Queen Mary

When at sea he enjoyed painting in his off duty hours, but most of all he loved his fishing. When he retired he would spend all day river or beach fishing, and when Ted was on leave, they would go off together night fishing as well, usually down on a beach.

Arthur was very impatient and a little impetuous, and on more than one occasion would have drowned if Ted had not been with him; he would get too near the waves, filling his sea boots up with water, or he'd fall off the rear end of the Sandbanks ferry, or get swamped at Warborough Bay.

Arthur's German Shepherd dog, Bella, was his constant companion when he actually sat down, and he would sit in his armchair for hours, with one hand on Bella's head and a book in the other, watching the old black and white TV at the same time.

When Sophie was a few days old, we took her to meet him. He was watching the wrestling, and sat proudly holding his new granddaughter in his arms. As the match heated up so did he, twisting and turning in his chair, nearly hurling the poor child at the screen in frustration. Woe betide you if you got in his line of vision.

I often paint old gentlemen like Arthur, with their dogs, hiding from their wives in sheds, fishing or causing mayhem.

Arthur understood my love of books and painting; we had the greatest respect for each other.

TED

My husband Ted is the inspiration for my fisherman paintings. He has always been a keen fisherman, be it river, beach, or from a boat. This photograph is of Ted aged about three seeing if he can catch anything in a bucket.

Ted went into the Merchant Navy in 1943 just a few weeks after his 16th birthday. He left home early one foggy November morning, boarded the train at Parkstone, near Poole, and journeyed to Waterloo. There he joined a number of other young fellows and they crossed London to get the train to Greenock, Scotland.

Having arrived at their destination, Ted and some of the other boys joined the crew of the RMS *Queen Elizabeth*, which was in service at that time as a troop carrier, going across the Atlantic to New York as a hospital ship and returning to Britain with fresh fighting troops. Many a war bride also travelled to her new home in America, and many a war bride came back a bit later on the same ship.

Once Ted was on board, he was given two buckets – one to put chewing gum in, that had to first be scraped off the deck, and the other to be sick in, which in Ted's case proved to be very useful. Some weeks later he dispensed with the second bucket, having been told by an old hand at sea that to cure his seasickness he should eat Hershey chocolate bars. The cure worked, and he spent the next nineteen years at sea with no ill effects, other than an occasional over indulgence of Captain Morgan's rum.

Having sailed on the *Queen Elizabeth* during and just after the war ended, Ted also did a few trips on the *Aquitania* and the *Queen Mary*.

In 1949 he joined the *Caronia* on her maiden voyage. She was a new Cunard liner, built strictly for cruising and was also known as 'The Green Goddess' because she was so lovely. For the next fourteen years Ted sailed on her.

The *Caronia* had just had her annual overhaul in November 1960 and was due to sail the day after Christmas for a five month cruise, when Ted's father was taken seriously ill, so he decided to stay at home and re-join the ship in the summer for the North Cape cruise.

It was during his time at home that Ted invited me out … to go fishing.

I should have known what was to come. Whenever he was home on leave over the next few years we would go fishing, and in all weathers. Can you imagine anything more romantic than sitting in the pouring rain on a damp river bank or on Chesil Beach, with soggy bacon sandwiches to eat and cold tea from a flask? I can … the aroma of half-dead rag worms and mackerel is something I will never forget!

The result … we were married on the 31st of March 1967 at St Mary's Church, Ferndown, so I suppose there must be something to be said for it!

Becoming a first time father at the age of forty was a bit of a shock to Ted, but he took to it well. First there was Kait, then there was Sophie and then there was Ben.

We can't help laughing when we look at the two photos here, one of Ted admiring a fish and the other of him lovingly admiring our new born infant, Ben.

He is showing as much care in handling both of them ... at least he didn't throw Ben back!

Ted loved being a father and he also enjoyed being a granddad to our increasing 'clutch of grandchildren'.

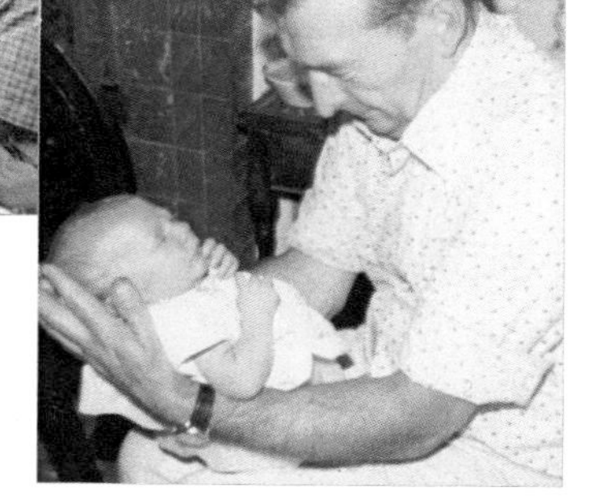

He was a quiet, wise granddad, and if the grandchildren sat down next to him on the old settee to watch a Western on the television, he would tell them all sorts of tales about his time at sea, some funny, some scary, especially the ones about dreadful storms. He was a good story teller.

KAIT

Catherine Suzan, our eldest daughter, who is known as 'Kait', was born three weeks early, after I spent a day running around on snow-covered ground trying to find the workman supposedly working on a problem in our road.

Kait has always been artistic and likes to live life her way. She had her own ideas on school uniform and hair colouring, and for some unknown reason got away with it, maybe because she was well behaved. She has a great sense of humour, which is essential in our family.

She is a strict vegetarian, and her absolute love of any animal, big or small, is famous. She took up hairdressing with my father's encouragement, and now has a mobile hairdressing business. Her pockets are always full of biscuits when she visits a pet owner.

Kait married briefly a few years ago, but her free spirit stepped in and she now lives with her two King Charles Cavalier dogs, Alfie and Amber, one quiet and one as mad as a hatter – a bit like Kait.

Girls like Kait appear in my paintings as tall, often glamourous, blondes, usually accompanied by equally glamorous dogs, such as salukis or greyhounds, and quite oblivious to the attention they are attracting.

SOPHIE

Sophie Alexandra, our younger daughter by 23 months, is the maternal one, and always said she would have a large family, which she has. Robyn is her eldest, next came Jordan, then Georgi, and last of all, Joe. Sophie loves them all equally and they are all a credit to her.

Sophie was nearly seven years old when Ben was born at the end of the hot summer of 1976, and she helped to look after him when I had to be in the bar ... apart from when he had whooping cough, making him dreadfully sick, a thing she cannot bear to this day – a bit of a problem when the children have the odd tummy bug. Sophie is a home lover and also likes her animals, having 'Hardy' the house rabbit, and 'Chief', her beautiful golden cocker spaniel. She loves her music and dancing; to get her off the dance floor is almost impossible.

Robyn

Jordan

Georgi

Sophie with Joe

Sophie inspires me in my family paintings of mothers surrounded by children of all ages, some looking out of the painting with knowing expressions, others making faces at each other – and very often they are are showing more more sense than the adults.

Likewise, the children in my paintings often closely resemble family members – where better to get inspiration?

BEN

Benjamin Edward, or 'Ben' as he is known, was a large, fun loving, easy going, kind child, who was happy so long as he had his toy cars and a bicycle. I had to have a strict routine with him, which I hadn't had with the girls, as it was only Ted and me running the pub. He slept in the bedroom above the jukebox and the dartboard, but he never had a problem sleeping, even with all the noise. It could also account for his appreciation of 70's music.

Ben has always enjoyed sport and grew into a six foot four inches tall, fun loving, easy going and kind man. He and his lovely wife, Lucy, are the proud parents of Ethan, who has the most remarkable pair of vivid blue eyes.

Although very patient, Ben doesn't suffer fools gladly and can get really mad if something strikes him as unfair, unkind or disrespectful. For many years Ben worked with people with brain injuries, and he is now making a success of his gardening business.

My family, being all so vastly different, make good models for my paintings, although Ted has been known to object to some of the poses I asked him to take up.

Because of his height and build, Ben is a good character to put in my work, ideal as a sporty sort of fellow, jogging, swimming or kayaking, and sometimes attracting appreciative looks from the ladies and disapproval from their companions.

LIVING IN BURLEY

We moved in 1985, family plus dog, to Burley, in the New Forest, in order to be near my father and stepmother, Mary. My father had an unusual sense of humour, and three weeks before our removal day from The Swordsman, he died. Had he been aware of the coincidence, he would have been highly amused.

We ran the Burley Club and lived in the flat above. When Ted retired in 1992 we stayed in the village, and I have been able to concentrate fully on my art ever since.

Our 'children' are all grown up now, leading their own lives and living not too far away, with their families and animals. We are a close family and I find inspiration from them all, even with the sometimes hair-raising reports of what they are doing.

In Burley there is always something to get involved in. It was a standing joke with the family that whenever I arrived home from some meeting or another, Ted would ask, "Well, what have you said yes to now?" More often than not it would incorporate something to do with art, such as scenery for the Burley Players' pantomime, a Christmas or Easter card for the church, posters for all sorts of happenings, helping the YOBs (Youth of Burley) paint the windows of the church room ready for Easter or Christmas, or designing the face of the Queen's Jubilee clock that now stands in the centre of the village.

One job that I have taken on in the village that doesn't involve art, is that of 'The Bouncer' on the door at the Women's Institute, where my experience as a pub landlady comes in handy. I can spot a mischief maker a mile off, not that there are any in our WI, but you never know … we haven't always been well behaved matrons, we could show the youngsters a thing or two.

The painting below is based on an event that happened many years ago. A friend, Lynn, called in for a chat, and as she was leaving she called out to Ted, "Goodbye, Ted" – but neither he heard nor answered her, he was so engrossed watching John Wayne save the day … yet again! My friend said, "Don't worry, I've got one of those at home."

Brother ROBIN

Sophie, Robin, baby Ben, Barbara, Kait and Ken

Ted and I had just returned to his parents' house, after yet another romantic day fishing, or rather Ted fishing and me looking after the worms and administering bacon sandwiches and tea at regular intervals, when my mother-in-law, Kit, greeted us with the news that my stepfather Ken had just phoned. He said that my brother Robin had been born unexpectedly, five weeks prematurely, and thankfully the baby and my mother were doing well, although a bit shocked.

I must admit that after being the only girl in the family, I was relieved it was still the case. I have always been proud of my three brothers, even though Paul, David and I fought like cats and dogs at times, when young.

Kait and Robin

Robin was born when our mother was 46. He was a most beautiful baby with dark eyes and dark hair, taking after his father Ken. To have such a baby was a novelty for our mother, as Paul, David and I had all been fair and blue-eyed as babies.

Robin, our 'baby' brother, is a contemporary of Paul's daughters, Angela and Birgit, and of David's children, Ian, Zoe, Oliver and James, and my children, Kait, Sophie and Ben, who think of him more as another brother, than as an uncle.

My mother and Ken took the tenancy of The Pembroke Arms, at Fovant, when Robin was a young boy. During the school holidays and if we could arrange cover for the bar, we would pick Robin up and take him with us for a day out.

Our ventures out usually ended up with Kait and Ben being car sick and Sophie threatening to jump out of the car as she cannot bear anyone being sick.

Robin was always the best behaved. He was a gifted child, especially mathematically, and even at a young age was in great demand as a 'scorer' when there was a darts match, as he was quicker than any player.

He was always laughing, having our mother's attitude to life, but like his father, his humour can be wicked and he has a rare turn of phrase. He studied hard at school and university, and kept a close eye on his widowed father.

Robin and his wife, Claude, live in St Albans with their two sons, Jacob and Samuel. Unlike yours truly, Robin is a keen cyclist, and when not working hard on his marketing business, he goes off on cycling journeys, sometimes hundreds of miles long.

Our mother still kept her dogs when Robin was a boy and they were great company for him as he grew up, especially Winston, the Golden Labrador.

When our brother David died, Robin and his family asked if they could 'adopt' his gun dog, 'Tug', that he had bred.

It was quite a change for Tug to now live in an urban area, rather than the Dorset countryside, but he settled down to retirement, only occasionally letting the side down, as when Robin took him to a country park where Tug came out of the undergrowth with a pheasant in his jaws. Because Tug had spent so much time on shoots with David and getting wet, it is no wonder he has arthritis.

Jacob and Samuel, adore Tug. It's a special relationship – a bit like the one my mother and father had with their dog 'Ginny'.

Robin, Samuel and our son, Ben, are fans of Bournemouth Football Club and sometimes meet up for a Bournemouth football home match.

Our cousin Elizabeth, also a keen supporter, goes independently to the game and has her own seat away from them – a wise decision, as sometimes Robin and Ben's colourful remarks and opinions might not be suitable for a lady's ears.

The thing I love about Robin is his ability to have everyone in stitches laughing, and his kindness.

THE FISHERMAN

I suppose it's not surprising that there's often a fisherman in my paintings – after all, I've spent more days than I could count lying on a river bank or sitting on a harbour wall, with my pencils and paper, sketching.

But when it's raining ... that might be a time a fisherman and his dog want to be on their own.

On the Christmas before we were married Ted gave me an extra special gift … a fork for digging bait. He was rather concerned that the fork I had been using was too heavy for me. He was always so thoughtful.

The fork is still in use 48 years later, mainly for digging in the garden.

In the picture you can see it sticking out of the barrow of soil, while guess who gets on with the gardening.

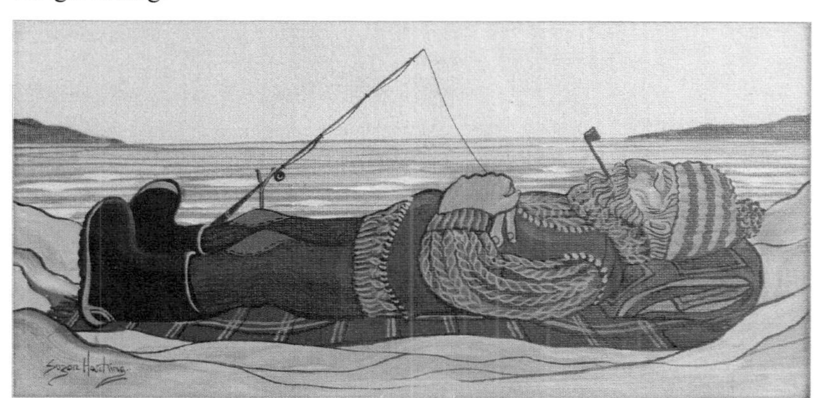

Isn't this every man's idea of bliss – peace, a pipe and a slack fishing line.

But it's not always that simple … and when the family is about … ?

One day when our children were small, we were were fishing at Hengistbury Head, and I took the children off for some ice cream.

On our return, we found Ted clutching his hand, which was bleeding. He had caught and been stung by a weever fish.

To get rid of the poison he had cut his hand with his fishing knife.

No harm done … he still has two hands.

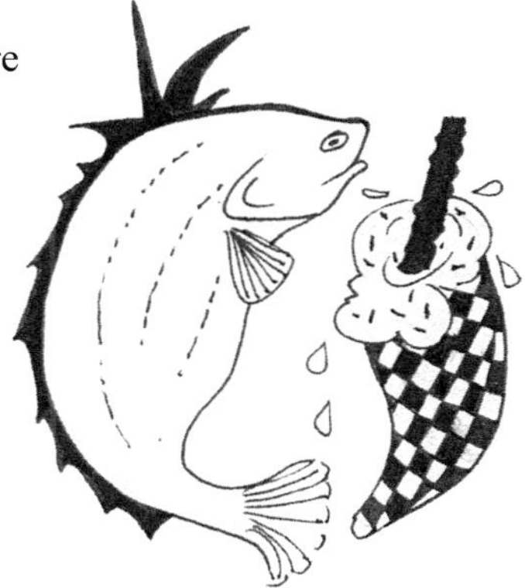

WEST BAY

Ted and I spent many happy times at West Bay over the years – our honeymoon, family holidays, fishing trips, birthdays and anniversaries, but in recent times, after several dramas, accidents, arguments, and the loss of a family dog, I began to wonder if West Bay would rather we stayed away.

One year we visited specifically for me to make some 'harbour' drawings for a commissioned painting.

It was only when we reached our hotel room overlooking the harbour, that we discovered our window, which I hoped to work from, was covered in scaffolding. I could only just see tiny chinks of the scene through the criss-cross of poles and planks.

Another time, shortly after our arrival, we had to return home immediately for Ted to go into hospital for a gall stone operation.

Yet another time, Ted and I were celebrating our wedding anniversary at West Bay and, after a brisk walk around the harbour, we went into our favourite pub – Ted tripped, breaking his nose and hurting his wrist. I think the blood stains are still on the flagstones to this day. The ambulance was called, but Ted declined their offer of taking him to hospital.

The following day, our daughter, Sophie, took him to A&E and, true to form, he was spectacularly car sick.

Still undeterred, we then planned a further family holiday at West Bay, which had to be delayed by a few days as Ted developed pneumonia a couple of weeks before we were due to go. In spite of wind and rain, we had a good time. Ted stayed indoors to rest, but one day sneaked off on his own, ate a large 'all day breakfast' and suffered from painful indigestion all day.

The look on Ted's face on getting home relatively unscathed was indescribable. After that no one dared to suggest a return visit on the next year – one of Ted's glowering stares was enough to stop the bravest soul in their tracks.

I still love West Bay.

THE BOAT TRIP

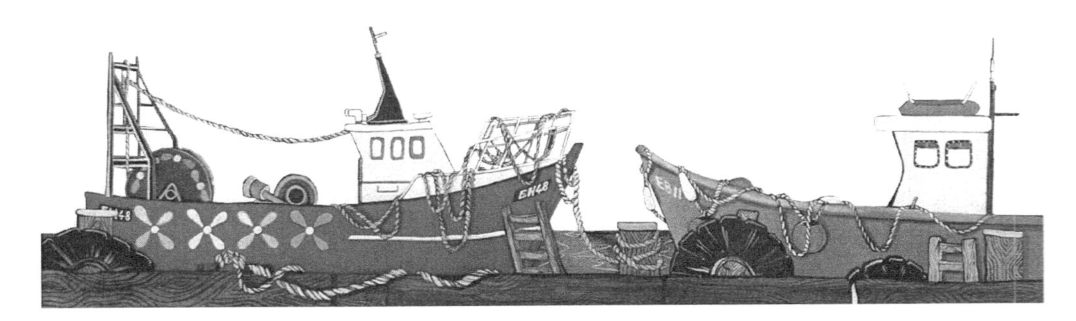

This painting idea had been rattling around my head for many years, ever since an event took place whilst on holiday in Weymouth. Our son Ben was about thirteen at the time and Ted suggested that the three of us take a boat trip around Portland Harbour. Rather than go shopping with our daughters, Kait and Sophie, plus their friend Justine, which could have proved fatal to my purse, I decided, to everyone's surprise and against my better judgement, to go with Ted and Ben. I overcame my misgivings and we took our seats amongst a coach load of unusually large ladies and their husbands, and waited for the boat to set off.

I was a bit taken aback when the skipper announced that there was a problem with our boat, saying another would be brought alongside and that we were to transfer into it … carefully.

During his time at sea, Ted had assisted on many an occasion with passengers and launches going to and fro from the *Caronia* as they travelled the world, so he stood up and offered to help the 'ladies' climb from one boat to the other. Another obliging chap also helped, and all went well until the two boats began to slowly drift apart. "Not to worry," said Ted afterwards, "she was wearing huge bloomers, they would have kept her afloat had she fallen in."

ADRIFT

I belong to various art groups and societies, including the Romsey Art Group, of which I have been a member for over forty-four years. I also belong to the Burley Art Group, the New Forest Art Society, the Ringwood Art Society, and am proud to be one of the founder members of The Woodlanders. I was a member of the Bournemouth Art Club, but it was hard to attend when Ted was ill. I have been told I can re-join and I would like to do so in time.

The Woodlanders have been in existence for twenty-five years now, and every year we hold an exhibition in the Burley Village Hall – eight artists, two potters and two woodcarvers, along with the New Forest Woodcarvers, who also exhibit with us. Every year, after our exhibition, we make a donation to Diabetes UK, a favourite charity of mine, having been a Type 1 diabetic for nearly forty years.

Last summer, for the monthly meeting of the Ringwood Art Society, it was arranged for the local camera club to come along to talk about our paintings from a photographer's point of view, while we provided an artist to talk about the photographs from an artist's viewpoint. Members of the art society and the camera club were asked to each bring along a piece of work for the 'appraisal', the subject being 'water' as I recall.

I took along my rather stylised painting of four boats, three safely in the shallows and the fourth heading out to sea. The painting was on quite a large box canvas and painted in my favourite bright primary colours. The camera club critic looked at my painting and said he felt the fourth boat should be removed as in his opinion it spoiled the composition. I didn't take any notice, even a fellow artist said, "Leave it alone." When it came to the Annual Exhibition I submitted the boat painting as it was and was delighted to be awarded the trophy for the 'most original painting'. We all see things differently and, as my mother-in-law, Kit, used to say, "You can always stand aside and enjoy your own opinion."

BEACH

One summer's day during the school holidays when we were living at the farm, my parents, brothers and I, were enjoying a day on Sandbanks beach. The boys were in the sea playing with an old, patched, inflated inner tube that had belonged to a big tractor tyre, splashing about, pushing each other into the water and having a great time. They thought they were the 'bee's knees' with the large black monstrosity, and none of us questioned why other children had brightly coloured water wings and safety floats.

I was busy burying my sleeping father in the sand, when suddenly I spotted our 'Uncle Jack' walking along the water's edge, holding the hand of a pretty young lady. At eight years old you don't have a lot of tact, and before anyone could stop me, I ran over to them, shouting at the top of my voice, "Hello Uncle Jack, what are you doing here? Mummy and Daddy are over there, do you want to come and see them?"

He looked at me in horror and waved me away, explaining to his companion that it was clearly a case of mistaken identity, he had no idea 'who this child belongs to'.

When I went back to my parents, my mother said he'd had a lucky escape, as Auntie Zona wasn't with us, having stayed at home with her new actor friends … hmm … ?

BEACH HUTS

Beach huts and promenades are a favourite subject, and just to sit and watch the world go by, pen in hand, sketchbook on my knee, a crab sandwich and a mug of tea close by, is bliss. Beach huts are fun whatever the weather, and our family, young and old, have spent many days at the seaside 'playing house' in one. Mind you, sitting in a beach hut, watching the rain pour down outside as my husband Ted fished, with only an old newspaper full of rag worms for company, can strain the best of relationships. I am always amazed at how, even with the closeness of huts, the occupants manage to keep themselves to themselves, making sure they don't go over the invisible boundaries of their neighbours' space. Over the years I have accumulated many drawings of things that go on in these small individual spaces. One thing that makes me laugh is how, even in this age of mountains of flesh on show generally, people are excruciatingly shy when changing on the beach, another reason to bless the beach hut.

COAST

My sketch books are full of drawings, notes and ideas for boat and beach paintings. I love the shape, colour and complexity of seaside towns and harbours, complete with their assortment of boats, people, houses and cottages.

As you can see from the sketch opposite, my early experiences of colouring in the scribbled shapes that my mother drew for me can still be seen. I love patterns and curves, and blocks of colour.

The coastlines in Hampshire, Dorset and the West Country are perfect … and they're full of people doing all sorts of things.

When sitting to sketch or paint, there is time to see and hear what is going on.

To the left is a purely imaginary painting, drawn from memories of still days when the little boats far out in the bay need to tack hard to sail a course, and when you can hear from the distance the sound of children playing with their dog in a field and the cries of seagulls following the tractor's plough.

The rooks in the field of corn have found out that the scarecrow doesn't move, but they're still keeping a careful distance, just in case ...

NEEDLES

As children we would be taken to Sandbanks for a day on the beach and, until I nearly drowned at the age of nine, I was happy going in the water. Since then it's been the safety of sandcastles and beach huts for me.

Even though I don't swim, I love to be at the beach, and not only on summer days.

Wiltshire is landlocked, and when we moved to The Swordsman, we all missed spending days by the water, so on every chance when we had the day off we headed to Bournemouth or, more especially, Hengistbury Head, with its added attraction of the land train, for when the children got fidgety I could take them off, leaving Ted to fish in peace.

I would grab the odd peaceful moment for my sketch books and fill them with quick thumb-nail drawings of all sorts of people, in all sorts of shapes and sizes, doing and eating all sorts of things.

There are some places along the coast opposite the Isle of Wight, where it looks as if it would be easy to just walk over to the island, and this painting portrays a grandfather holding in each hand a trusting grandchild, as they consider whether it would be possible to make the 'short journey' over to the Needles.

The pinstripe trousers are ancient survivors of the grandfather's demob. suit from decades ago.

THE WITCH

Burley has in the past been associated with witchcraft.

I have always rather liked witches … the nice sort of course … the ones who appear in children's books and get their spells wrong, and who are kind to their cats.

I imagine them in their houses by a good fire, enjoying a cosy chat like the rest of us. The witch in my painting has her rollers in, getting ready for a night out with the girls, while her husband settles down to a quiet tipple of his favourite Tarantula Blood, vintage 1654.

Many Burleyites would dispute whether there ever were, or are, witches in the village.

What's certain is that crowds of 'grockels' flood into Burley every summer, hoping to get a glimpse of one of its famous witches. It's good for trade and so the stories carry on.

Who knows the truth? I have a feeling that any self-respecting woman with magical powers would keep well away.

Recently I was asked to submit designs for a Jubilee clock for the village. The brief was for eight designs within the clock face, including a witch.

Some time later it became clear that 'she' was not perhaps a popular choice, and at the village show a few people spoke to me about 'her'. Later that afternoon I was standing with the crowd outside the draw tent.

My number was drawn ... I had won a large broomstick.

A friend, sitting on a shooting stick, asked, "Are you flying home on that?"

"No," I said, "I only do that after dark."

"Oh," he replied, "I bet you say that to all the boys."

The design was altered at a later date to everyone's satisfaction.

The clock duly took its place in the village centre in spring 2014.

I like to think the inclusion of the red deer in full antler would have met the approval of the 'Monarch of the Forest', the famous stag of Burley, whose 16 year reign ended when he was shot by poachers in March of the same year.

As for the Burley witch ... well she is there too, and you can see what she is thinking.

BURLEY GROCKELS

When we lived above the Burley Club, I would sit in my 'eagle's eyrie' at the top of the outside staircase leading to our flat and have a wonderful view of the village centre. I could spend hours there with my sketchbook and pen, just soaking up images and getting ideas for my paintings.

If you've ever come here in the summer, you would know that Burley is a hot spot for visitors to the New Forest. They arrive in droves … in cars, off coaches and buses, on bikes, or just walking. Many people, not used to the Forest way of life, are taken aback when they see ponies roaming at will all over the village. They don't realise it is their right to do so, and that they haven't just escaped from a farmer's field.

Having travelled through the Forest, a 'townie' lady once asked me if the ponies were real, thinking they were all models, as in a theme park. Fortunately, most visitors have a better appreciation of the New Forest and all its ways.

Some of the 'holiday garbs' I saw from my staircase, were most unusual, and I felt then, as I do now, that there should be some limitations on 'corpulent gentlemen' in ill-fitting shorts, sporting socks and sandals, and maybe some of the lady visitors should have gone to a well-known opticians before reading size labels when buying their holiday T shirts.

I am treading on thin ice really, as on more than one occasion my husband has looked at one of my rig outs and said in a horrified voice, "You're not going out in that, are you?" I did draw the line recently at a pair of vivid purple trainers that a snooty salesman was trying to get me to buy, telling him I had my reputation as 'the Burley WI bouncer' to think of.

THE STUDIO

Some years ago, an artist friend, Sarah Lyn Sibley, suggested that it might be a good idea to set up a small studio in the village, and asked Colin Courtice and me if we would be interested. The three of us got together and rented a wooden building belonging to what was the ironmongers, standing next to the Burley Club car park.

We shared the space between us and came up with the bright idea of calling it 'The Studio'. Another artist, Mary Evans, joined us as a fourth 'studonian', and when Mary and her husband set sail for New Zealand, we invited the artist Brenda Farrell to come in with us.

It was great fun. There was only enough room for one of us to work at any given time, but we arranged a rota and hung our paintings on every spare space of wall, and were able to paint away to our hearts content, enjoying the interruption of friends and those visitors who braved their way out of the village centre, leaving the safety of the coach or car park, into the wilderness of Pound Lane – a long trek of fifty yards.

Our new visitors were pleasantly surprised and pleased to find us, and we all made some useful contacts, selling paintings, cards and prints, and accepting commissions.

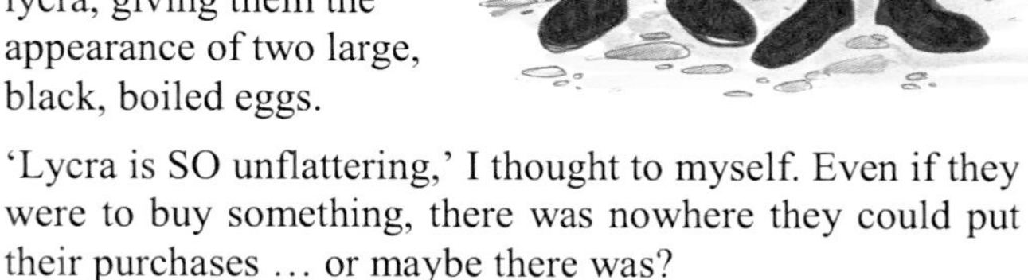

One very hot afternoon I was working on a painting that was nearing completion, when I heard the sound of footsteps crunching on the gravel outside the studio. I looked up … there stood two mature and extremely overweight cyclists, looking hot and sweaty to say the least. Neither the man nor the woman with him were in the first flush of youth, and they were both dressed from head to toe in tight, figure-hugging lycra, giving them the appearance of two large, black, boiled eggs.

'Lycra is SO unflattering,' I thought to myself. Even if they were to buy something, there was nowhere they could put their purchases … or maybe there was?

In time, because of various commitments, our little group of artists decided to call it a day and each work at home. It was shame, as many local people knew where we were and would pop in for a chat. We were there for nearly ten years and I still miss it, although the vision of that hot afternoon is something I am still trying to come to terms with.

THE WOODLANDERS

In 1990 a group of us got together, calling ourselves 'The Woodlanders', and put on an art exhibition at Burley Village Hall. It is now an annual event, and we know from our comment book that many people visit the New Forest to coincide with our exhibition in September, because they enjoy it so much.

Over the twenty-five years since our first exhibition, many fine artists, potters and woodcarvers have joined our group, and even though some no longer take part in our exhibitions, we still think of them as part of the 'Woodlander family'. Sadly, over the last few months three of our Woodlanders have gone off to the 'Big Studio in the Sky'; Diana Hawkins, my fellow co-founder member, Colin Courtice, who was with us from day one, and Brian Harrild – all well known and respected artists.

The Woodlanders Art Exhibition Preview, 1997

Back row: Colin Courtice, Brian Williams, Tony Mercier, Ron Milsom & Joe Wilding
Front row: Daphne Ellman, Diana Hawkins, Josie Berrow, Jan Milsom, Rosemary Grant, Buster Merryfield, Geraldine Taylor & Suzan Houching

Our Preview evenings have always been fun, and many interesting people have opened our exhibitions: Hannah Gordon, Carl Tyler, Charlie Dimmock, Richard Digance, Ian Pepperall, Julian Clegg, Buster Merryfield, Sylv Willoughby, Lawrie McMenemy, Janet Courtice, Sandi Jones, Murray Walker OBE, Richard Cartridge, Alina Jenkins and Simon Parkin. Some of these people have done the honours on more than one occasion, among them Hannah Gordon, who has also written the foreword for this book.

Not long ago, we asked Murray Walker if he would open our exhibition and he kindly agreed, but insisted that as the exhibition was in support of Diabetes U.K. he wanted nothing other than a homemade fruit cake for his trouble. Joyce Williams, whose husband, Brian Williams, is one of our woodcarvers who has been with us since our second exhibition, provided a splendid cake, which Murray was delighted with. Earlier that summer, on a painting afternoon I sketched some classic cars that belonged to Pam and Ian Mason Smith, and to go with the cake, I gave Murray a small painting of one of their cars – not a partaker of a Grand Prix I'm afraid, but I have found out from Tim Edgerton, who works for the National Motor Museum, that the car is a 1933 Austin 7 Box Saloon.

Murray Walker and Suzan

2015 is The Woodlanders' Silver Jubilee, and when I think of all the lovely people who have exhibited with us, and the wonderful back up we've received from all the 'honorary' members, from husbands, including Ted, wives, partners and families, I am very proud and grateful.

COMMISSIONS

My paintings are very often of a humorous nature, and I'm pleased to say they hang in many houses in Burley. One gentleman, Mike Allen, has nineteen of my paintings, far exceeding Lord Bath, who has five of my works in his private collection at Longleat.

I enjoy accepting commissions for all sorts of events, be they special birthdays, anniversaries, corporate events, or family occasions, such as weddings or christenings, and have lately been painting the odd landscape, which surprises some people, although they guess it is my work when they see it – maybe it's the colours I use. I think my linear style comes from the days before Ted and I married, when I worked for my friend Ruth at her 'Wimborne Pottery' as a decorator, using geometric designs and drawing on plates.

The painting below of the New Forest Cider open weekend was commissioned by Sue and Barry Topp. It depicts all things relating to cider making, as well as the Topp family who run their cider business in Burley. Sue and Barry are in the bottom right of the painting, their family on the left hand side, and their friends are portrayed throughout the picture. I painted this picture a few years ago, before the fundraising weekend included a display of Morris dancing, so the dancers are not shown, although they are now a regular feature, along with a variety of cider making machinery, country crafts, all sorts of interesting stalls and information about cider making.

THE PIPELINE CALENDAR

In 1994 ESSO were laying their pipeline through the New Forest and thanks to Mr Barry Rickman, the photographer from Sway, who put my name forward, I was commissioned to illustrate their calendar for the year in a humorous way, with the images all depicting something that 'might' happen, nothing too factual.

January is a street scene where all the ladies are pushing to get into the shops first as the sales are on. Some workmen are enjoying a tea break, reading the newspaper and studying form, all under the watchful eye of a small boy who is a little concerned about the man with a lighter!

It makes me think of an afternoon many years ago when I was at art school and some of us played truant, taking ourselves off to the cinema – that was when there was such a thing in Poole itself. The film showing was *A League Of Gentlemen* starring many well-known British actors, including Jack Hawkins, Nigel Patrick and Richard Attenborough. I loved it and still watch it if I get the chance.

There is a line where Jack Hawkins is asked by one of the 'team' if his wife is still alive. The answer is given with such venom and reminds me of my father on one of the rare occasions when he really lost it. The film is a little complicated and involves a bank robbery planned by a bitter ex-army chap. He is a clever man, but sadly the whole plan is ruined by a small boy collecting car numbers, of which one is his. Our sympathy was with the robbers and we all felt sorry they had been discovered thanks to a young child. The image of the child in the street, just watching, has always stayed with me ever since.

February finds a fisherman and his faithful dog sitting in the pouring rain in a forbidden spot on the bank of the river.

All hope is fading of catching anything, as the fish are using the pipeline to hide behind, out of danger of the fisherman's line. How long can they sit there? Is the pub open yet? Has her mother gone home?

March is the time when a wedding is taking place in the church, under which the pipeline has been laid. The vicar is a little worried as the best man and the bridegroom look as if there is a problem. Have the rings been dropped down the grille on top of the pipes? A lady guest is late in arriving to take her seat on the groom's side, maybe she was reluctant to attend for some reason?

A while ago I painted a picture of a bride running towards the church, where the bridegroom and guests were eagerly waiting for her. A friend and I were chatting recently about my work, and she said, "I remember a painting of yours where the bridegroom and guests were waiting at the church for the bride and she was running away in the opposite direction in great haste." ... same picture, different memory!

April In a fine spell between the showers a farmer's wife stands impatiently waiting for the cows to be milked. She needs a pail of milk in the kitchen, but the farmer is still trying to get the cows into the milking shed and they are not helping because they are far more interested in the gossiping rabbits who have been building their burrow under the edge of the field.

The men laying the pipes have kindly made a detour to avoid disturbing the bunnies.

Out at sea a tanker sails towards Fawley oil refinery.

May

The gym mistress has taken the children outside to the playground for their lesson, as it is such a lovely morning, but most of them are not paying attention as they are far more interested in what the digger is doing.

The workmen are digging a trench ready for more pipes to be laid. Let us hope the playing field will be left alone.

June

A family are picnicking here in what they thought was a quiet corner of the Forest. Father is putting up the wind break, but has been a bit too enthusiastic about hammering in the supporting poles and has hit the pipeline, resulting in a sudden jet of oil. Mother is horrified and so will the rest of them be when it lands on them. … another happy outing!

In real life, a family on a picnic in the New Forest will very often find a nice cosy spot and settle down, only for the Forest ponies to find them and put on their 'Oh, we're SO hungry' look.

However, it is an absolute 'NO-NO' to feed them, because it can be dangerous. More than a few visitors have found themselves in the A&E department thanks to a well-aimed hoof.

July

On the beach the children are busy building sandcastles and they've found that the pipeline makes a very good foundation.

Picnickers are all gathered there too – the knitters, the sun worshippers and the odd fisherman further along in a quieter spot.

Mother is keeping a close eye on father, who is supposedly reading a book on football … or is he?

August

This picture gives meaning to 'A Shotgun Wedding' – a term that was used many years ago, but is no longer relevant today … how things have changed!

A farmer is clutching his shotgun to his chest, searching for his wayward daughter and her boyfriend.

The pair are hiding in a pipe – one of a heap waiting to be lain in the trench that was being dug by the distant digger.

Now they are in danger on both sides, having been found by one of the farmer's dogs, who is about to give the game away.

The young man should have stuck to his work!

September, the month when my imagination took the pipeline under the sea where it has drawn the attention of various onlookers from the top of the cliffs. Two enthused professor types are having a heated argument about what it is out there in the water ... could it be the Loch Ness Monster?

Again there is a small boy listening intently, and as for the seated lady, who is with one of the gentleman, she is doing as my mother-in-law would have advised – 'standing aside and enjoying her own opinion'.

October and a baptism, where the vicar is hoping the crying infant will calm down so that he can get the ceremony over and hand the child back to its anxious parents. Not so – just as he is about to name the baby, he is shocked to discover it's good old ESSO oil spouting up from the font.

When our son was baptised in our church at Dinton, my father and stepmother arrived at the end of the service in a bit of a state. My father did not like cats, but as they left the house to come to us, they'd found a wounded cat beside their gate, covered in oil.

Thinking it was their cat, they rushed it to the nearest vet and ran up a hefty bill in the process, only to discover on their return home, their own cat basking in the sunshine. Who the other cat belonged to, no one knew.

November means Bonfire Night.

The bonfire has been built, the Guy is in place, dressed in old Tweed, and the fire is lit … over an oil pipe, which with the heat has burst and is sending up a jet of oil.

Look out everyone!

… I think this could get interesting!

December

Everyone in the office has finished their work and the Christmas party is in full swing. There is plenty to drink, maybe too much, and food to enjoy. Even Santa is having a fine time. Let us hope that not too many have hangovers in the morning and that when they meet again in the New Year all will be well.

BEAULIEU

In the early spring of 2001, I was ill with flu and feeling very sorry for myself. The telephone rang and it was Laura from the National Motor Museum, Beaulieu, asking me if I would be interested in taking on the job of painting a mural as a backdrop to a display of toy vehicles that was to be held in the Motor Museum a few weeks later as part of the 'Motoring Through Childhood' exhibition. I was only too pleased to be commissioned to do the work, and readily accepted.

Fired with enthusiasm I sketched out a shop full of toys that could be seen in the exhibition, except for one item that I put in for fun.

My start on the painting of this 20 x 8 foot mural coincided with the severe outbreak of foot and mouth disease, and people were asked not to travel across the Forest any more than was necessary. I anticipated that the mural would take the best part of two weeks, working all day. Fortunately, one of the men in the office at the Motor Museum was able to give me a lift there in the morning and a lift home when he had finished in late afternoon, enabling me to paint all day.

At the height of the outbreak the museum was closed voluntarily for a few days as a precautionary measure, but I was quite happy to carry on with my painting in the silent, empty hall on my own. I was working in the part of the museum overlooking the area where all the cars and vehicles were displayed … a great opportunity for sketching. It was perishing cold, because the museum was closed, so I was wearing multi-layered clothing, topped with an ancient, ancient, grey hoodie.

I was happily painting away on a bottom section one afternoon, when I heard a loud gasp of horror. I stood up, looked around, and there was a security man who had been checking that all was well. When he saw it was me, he laughed, saying he had forgotten I was there, and that I had looked like a headless monk … he thought at last he had seen a ghost.

The mural depicted toys and vehicles from the 1920s era up until the turn of the 21st century. On the left side, I painted a mature lady with a large bosom, looking like Mrs Bagshott, and dressed in a fur coat and pearls, similar to an auntie of *Just William* vintage. She was clutching her small handbag, out of which she was taking her purse to pay for the toy that her young charge had chosen.

The middle section showed a variety of toy vehicles on shelves, a smaller version of the Beaulieu veteran bus and a penny-farthing, with in the foreground a smart red pedal car being driven by the Honourable Ralph Montagu as I imagined he would have looked when a child.

On the right hand side a father is using his credit card to buy something for his assorted children.

I am not sure what happened to the mural, but I think it might have been painted over to give way for a new exhibition feature.

TIME PASSES

As the title suggests, this painting is all about the passage of time. The older couple are looking at the young man and his girlfriend, who are in a warm embrace. The older gentleman is a bit envious of their freedom … he could never have kissed his to-be-wife in their day … any more than holding hands and her father would have reached for his shotgun.

His wife of many years is a little more disapproving – sour grapes maybe – thinking of her days as a young gal.

The young couple are oblivious to anyone other than themselves, time means nothing to them.

The two schoolchildren find the situation amusing and slightly embarrassing, realising it won't be too many years until they will be having girlfriends and boyfriends, and by then the young people in front of them will have settled down and become boring like their parents.

The two bus timetables promise buses, but they are out of date – will a bus ever arrive?

There once was a fellow called Jim
Who married a girl on a whim
It's such a great pity
She was always so pretty
But now she's a large, not a slim.

WOOING

How Do You Do?

A young girl is introducing her latest boyfriend, a punk rocker, to her bemused parents. Maybe he is not the ideal choice they would have made for their precious daughter – even the Queen, whose speech they've been watching, looks a little dubious, but there we are.

Whose choice is it anyway?

Sometimes the most unlikely of 'paramours' turn out to be the best. My own parents were a little concerned when Ted and I married, because Ted was nearly seventeen years older than me, but we were together for almost forty-eight years of marriage.

In the painting below, a young man has risked taking his latest girlfriend home to meet his family. The small boy is trying to impart to the young lady some lurid details of his brother's previous relationships, whilst the older boy is probably kicking him under the table. Mother and father are just hoping that a 'possible incident' will go unnoticed by everyone.

Grandma has been asked to sit on a low stool, her chair having been given to the visitor. Her daughter-in-law is passing around the sandwiches, saying, "Come on Gran, you must eat to keep your strength up." Has Grandma forgotten her teeth or doesn't she care for whatever she is being offered? … the family dog does, and is quite happy to 'help Grandma out'.

WEDDINGS

In this painting the mother of the bride is putting the final touches to her daughter's veil, assuring her that she looks lovely. Her daughter is looking fondly at the photograph of the man she is to marry in less than an hour's time.

The father of the bride is sitting on the bed, twisting his hat in his hands, wondering how on earth all this is going to be paid for and hoping that his future son-in-law will prove to be a good husband to his eldest child.

The four younger children are making the most of the adults' lack of supervision and enjoying a good old pillow fight … and the box of delicious chocolates, carelessly left unattended. The family dog is up to his old tricks, chewing one of the bride's satin wedding shoes. He knows he shouldn't and that's why he is hiding.

Maiden aunt, Florrie, is keeping a look out for the wedding cars and reassuring herself that she has a handkerchief at the ready, as she is bound to start crying during the service.

Like most people, I have attended many a wedding over the years. This photo shows Ted and me on our way to the wedding of Ted's niece, Judy, at St Peter's Church, Bournemouth, in 1965. It's a pity that it's in black and white – I loved that blue polka dot dress.

Getting ready for a wedding seems to stir up a mixture of emotions. Like the couple in the picture below, you put on your best dress and hat, or for the men your smartest suit and tie, and look in the mirror remembering your own special day. What a shock when you realise all the years that have gone by … and with them a good number of the hopes and dreams you had when you were younger!

When we lived at Henbury Farm, Ron, a local young man who worked at the farm, was planning to get married and he asked our father if he would be his Best Man. My brothers and I couldn't believe how much time Daddy spent jotting down notes about what he was going to say about Ron and his bride. He certainly prepared!

It was only at the reception when he stood up to give his Best Man's speech, that everything went wrong. We children weren't invited to the wedding (I wonder why?) but according to Mummy the speech went well until he said, "… and I hope Ron will be very happy with Joan." With that poor Ron put his head down and started to cry … his bride's name was not Joan.

THE RECEPTION

A pretty bride, sunshine and a lovely country garden – what could possibly go wrong?

The weddings I have been to, apart from one or two that will stay nameless, have all been lovely, full of happiness, love fun, laughter, and a couple of times … drink.

My parents divorced two weeks short of twenty-five years of marriage and both went on to remarry. In my mother's case it was to Ken, who was a real character and proved to be a good friend, as well as an hilarious stepfather.

Some years later, our father decided to ask Mary, a lady that he had met when he moved to Brockenhurst to help his parents, to marry him. At 3pm on June 12th, the day before his birthday, we gathered in St Nicholas Church, Brockenhurst, awaiting the 'Bride and Groom' for their church blessing. The door of the church flew open and a shrill voice of my four year old nephew, Ian, rang out as he ran into church, "Oh no, not another bloody wedding." Apparently his dad, David, and family had already been to a friend's wedding that morning!

One member of the congregation wasn't feeling too well, having overdone the pre-wedding drinks, but she behaved well and was not the only one sporting a splitting headache! My brother Paul, who was stationed in Germany at the time, had been able to get leave to come home for the wedding, and not having seen him for a few months, our father was so pleased he could be with us, as we all were. We had met up at The Cat and Fiddle the night before and were all 'in good spirits' literally. I remember consuming more than I should have done of the lethal 'draught sherry' that came in wooden casks and tasted great … at the time of consumption. Naturally we all celebrated in style, only to feel rather jaded the following morning. Even our father looked a pale shade of green in the cold light of day.

THE TRADITIONS

Weddings are full of traditions, and what's more important than the cake? When everyone is full up … of food, and drink, and speeches, in comes … the CAKE!

Once in a while when we were at The Swordsman, Ted and I would be asked to take on a wedding reception. They were quite hard work as it was just the two of us, but we enjoyed doing them, calling in help from a couple of friends.

At one such occasion, our son Ben, then aged about five, was under the tender care of his sisters. They were playing in our garden with some children that belonged to the wedding party, when Ben ran across our lawn and tripped, falling over and hurting his elbow. Emergency!

There was no way Ted could leave the bar, so the S.O.S went out to a couple of retired ex -licence friends, who lived nearby. Gwen offered to stand in for me and help Ted behind the bar, and her husband took Ben and me to Salisbury Hospital. Not only was Ben in a lot of pain and a bit fearful of what was going to be done (the X-ray showed that his elbow was cracked), but he was also rather confused … not because of the accident, but because of the other people who were waiting for attention.

Nearby that afternoon, there had been a re-enactment of a Cavalier and Roundhead battle, and afterwards four of the Cavaliers had crammed themselves into a Mini to drive home. On their way they crashed and ended up in casualty, the four of them sitting there, dressed in lacy shirts, waistcoats, long curling hair, breeches and boots, covered in mud and caked in blood from head to foot. Fortunately, they weren't too badly hurt … most of the mud was real, but a lot of the gore was suspect, and their wigs were a little askew.

CHRISTENINGS

Our family christenings have all run quite smoothly over the years, without too many hiccups, although there was the occasion of our eldest grandson's baptism when our then vicar, Alan Clarkson, was about to name him with the wrong name … it sounded similar, but it was not the one his parents had chosen for him. Fortunately, our daughter and her husband were quick thinking and they leant over and whispered loudly, "No, it's 'Jordan'."

My brothers, Paul and David, and I were baptised in our turn in Sturminster Marshall church, and on each occasion our father missed the ceremony, much to our mother's annoyance. He wasn't very keen on these gatherings and blamed the fact that he had to supervise the afternoon milking of the sixty dairy cows, or some other farm duty.

Most importantly, he is not in the photographs, which made our mother more than a little cross.

I have used these photographs, especially the one of my brother David's christening, as inspiration for more than one painting of people gathered together outside a church on special family occasions.

Centre: Barbara, David, Paul - Zona, Rene holding Suzan

Hovell's Cottage

When we were young children we were invited, along with our parents, to the baptism of another David, a little boy called 'David Applin'. His father and our father had known each other for many years and were rivals as National Hunt jockeys. David, his sister and his parents lived in 'Hovell's Cottage' in Henbury Park, the very same cottage that Paul and I had been born in. Everyone was gathered around the font, including my brother David and me, and the baby was duly baptised, but as the plug was pulled out of the font and the water gurgled away, it made David and me start to giggle uncontrollably. Our father told us to leave the church and to wait outside, as we couldn't be trusted to behave, even in a church …

This was typical of David and me. I was born on 12th February 1944, and David was born on 15th April 1945, and what with all that was going on – our mother's illness, the farm, and our father's horse racing – it was easier to treat us as twins.

We were nearly always referred to as 'the little ones' and if there was some trouble brewing, it usually involved the pair of us. Looking back, Paul was much better behaved.

David sadly died on August 4th 2011, of stomach cancer, and I still miss my fellow conspirator and our hilarious evening phone calls. When we were young, David definitely would have been the boy hanging on the font in the picture on the opposite page … and I? … I expect I would have put him up to pinching the chocolate biscuits and bringing them under the table for a secret party, like the little boy in the painting below.

BUMP

I like mirror images, and that is the basic idea behind this painting. Two pregnant mothers have bumped into each other outside the school at home time. Are they friends or foes?

We moved to our pub, 'The Swordsman', in Dinton, Wiltshire, two weeks before Christmas, and four weeks later, Kait started at school in the village. It proved to be a lovely school, but a new home and a new school in so short a time was a little daunting for her.
She was very fortunate to meet Becki, another new girl, and they struck up a friendship that has lasted to this day. Becki's mother, Eileen, and I also became friends, and still are over forty years later. We often laugh about things that happened all those years ago.

In time Sophie joined Kait at the school, and one afternoon when Sophie was about seven, it so happened that Eileen went to school to collect Becki early because she had a dental appointment. Going around the side of the building, Eileen met Sophie coming out of the ancient girls' loos, looking most indignant.

"Oh dear," said Eileen. "Whatever is the matter?"

To which Sophie replied, "I've just had my mouth washed out with soap, for swearing."

"Oh dear," said Eileen. "What was it like?"

To which Sophie answered, "It was bloody awful."

In the 'Bump' painting, Sophie is the child standing rather sheepishly behind the teacher, Kait is the child waiting for the gate to open, and Ben is the boy shouting, "Hoorah! It's time to go home."

MATERNITY

Our mother's health was not good after her bout of TB and she needed help with three boisterous children and a home to run, so a girl was recruited to live in. She came to stay with us, along with her baby, straight from a maternity home for unmarried mothers, and a few months later she moved with us to Henbury Farm, Daddy taking over the running of the farm as Granddad and family had moved to Brockenhurst. Not long after the move, the girl met and fell in love with the young man who worked with the horses, and they married, going on to raise a family of their own in addition to the first baby.

Next came another girl from the same maternity home and after being with us for a couple of weeks, she arranged to visit her friends at the home, some of whom were still awaiting the birth of their babies, knowing that they would more than likely have to make the difficult decision about adoption – a decision, thanks to my parents, that she didn't have to make. I was allowed to go with her on the bus. I was eight at the time, and aware that the girls in the 'home' were referred to as being 'in trouble', but no one thought to explain to me exactly what they had done that was so terrible. This girl and her baby stayed with us for six months, and every Sunday afternoon a tall skinny man would appear on a motorbike to spend time with them. Eventually, the girl's parents allowed her to take her baby home to live, as she and her young man planned on marrying. One morning she loaded up the large pram with baby and suitcases, and I walked with them to the end of the lane on their way to catch the train.

The outcome was different with the next young mother and one evening, having had enough of us, she told us what awful children we were. I don't know if this had any bearing on it, but shortly afterwards she decided that her baby was to be adopted, and off they both went, never to be heard of again. After this my parents found Ilsie, and it's lucky they did. If she hadn't been on hand to rescue me from drowning, I wouldn't be writing this today.

CLASH OF THE TITANS

An ordinary High Street on an ordinary day, with a café, a charity shop and the hairdressers … the pavement is crowded, as two busy mothers with pushchairs and children advance towards each other. Who will give way?

Again, I used family pets in the painting; 'Ping' our red Dachshund (mother of Percy, the partner in crime of Gertie, our Boxer), and Noni, a lovely gentle Dalmatian, who sadly developed bone problems after a confrontation with a neighbour's car.

There must have been previous ‘stand-offs’ as the child in the red jumper is wary of the child in the blue buggy.

The two boys in charge of their respective dogs are unaware of what is happening. One boy is making sure his dog doesn’t take his bag of sweets, and the other boy, with Ping, is looking at the man in the dark suit. Has he just been told off by him? The man’s wife, clutching flowers, looks as if she is about to say something – probably, “Leave the child alone.”

THE SINGING LESSON

My younger brother David and I were still attending Southlands School in Broadstone, when our elder brother Paul had moved on to Queen Elizabeth's Grammar School in Wimborne. Our headmistress at Southlands, Mrs Barnard, a formidable lady who I remember always used to wear green and dark brown, decided that the school would give a concert for the parents.

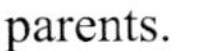

One afternoon, we children formed a long line and one by one we stood next to the piano, played by the aforementioned Mrs Barnard, and were instructed to sing a couple of bars individually.

As usual David and I were messing about and neither did very well.

At the end of these 'auditions' it was announced that five children would NOT be taking part in the concert. Guess who two of the five were!

I can imagine how mortified our parents must have been to see their children sitting on a bench alongside a wall, set apart from the choir.

Having been told in no uncertain manner that I ‘couldn’t sing’, had a profound effect. I still think that I sing out of tune, and when I am in church I am happy if there is a large congregation, as I then think no one will notice if I sound like a bear in labour.

I have painted two versions of ‘The Singing Lesson’ and our children appear in both at various ages. Our daughters, Kait and Sophie, were both in the church choir when we had our pub in Dinton, along with Kait’s friend Becki, but I am not entirely convinced that they contributed a lot to the singing.

Our vicar, Canon Treasure, must have been at his wits end at times with our family. One particular day I hurried up to the church for the ‘end of term service’ taking Ben, then aged two, with me.

Kait and Sophie had recently been telling Ben about witches and wizards, in a sisterly fashion of course. As Ben and I hurried up the path to the church door, Canon Treasure stepped out from behind a large oak tree. He was a very tall, big man, a little intimidating to a two-year-old, and he was wearing a black hat and a long black cloak … Ben froze. He refused to move.

Canon Treasure was most apologetic and said as he moved away, “Mrs Houching, if your little boy isn’t happy during the service, please feel free to take him out.” As it happened I never even got him INTO church that day!

JUST LOOK AT HER

Just Look at Her! There she goes!

An average High Street on yet another average day – a glamorous young woman is walking away from her favourite boutique, carrying a variety of luxury items that she has just purchased. She is accompanied by her snooty, equally glamorous dog. Two matron ladies are laden down with bags of mundane shopping, and with them is their rather overweight Boxer dog (Gertie again). The ladies are building up to boiling point, one of them will finally explode and say something catty – the look they give each other says it all.

The young woman has caught the attention of others too; a window dresser is watching with envy and a little sadness as she puts a display together, knowing full well that she cannot afford such luxury herself, and in the greengrocer's a husband is meant to be assisting his wife, but is far more interested in the young lady than choosing raspberries.

DOG WALKERS

Dogs have always played an important part in my life since I was a child, and I am now a 'batty old granny' but I still enjoy the company of our family dogs, even though Ted and I did not have one after Josie's demise. Each dog from over the years is remembered fondly for various reasons, whether it is their loyalty, affection, their beauty, intelligence, or in the case of our Boxers, their sense of humour.

Dogs are capable of so much, especially their work with the blind and deaf, and what would the military and the police do without them? I know of more than one romance that has started when two people have been introduced by their pets, as in the picture below. And many a man, woman or child, when they find life difficult, have found their sanity saved by their faithful dog. The gentleman in this picture has just retired and finds sanctuary in his garden shed with his understanding companion, away from 'her indoors'.

SPIDERS

My dislike of spiders is thanks to my lovely brother David ... once again! It was the year before we moved to Henbury Farm and we were living in an old Edwardian house in Broadstone. In one room was a bay window and a raised floor, making it ideal as a stage. We had put on a short 'Western' play for our parents. Paul was the sheriff and David was the 'bad man' who was shot and dragged off to Boot Hill ... not surprising considering Paul was writer, producer and casting director. I was given the role of saloon girl.

I should have known better, even at that age, but having taken our bows, I sat down in the small nursing chair. Whilst lying on the floor David had picked up a half-dead crane fly, and as I tilted my head backwards and laughed, he dropped the creature into my mouth, clamping my jaws shut. It's a good job he could run faster than me. What a lovely trio we were!

In this painting the little boy is about to frighten the living daylights out of the young girl, as he stands brandishing a spider, while she is daydreaming. Another example of brotherly love!

MORE SPIDERS

Even after Ted and I no longer had a dog, or any pet living the house, there were, and still are, a variety of family pets to look after when needed. I often put them in my paintings, but one creature that I WOULD NOT paint was 'Fangora', our eldest daughter Kait's pet tarantula, that she kept for 'company' when living in Southampton. Fangora, like all of her kind, periodically shed her skin by lying on her back; the skin would split and she could pull herself out, leaving behind a perfect, hollow case.

Ted and I were visiting Kait one evening and in the middle of cutting my hair, Kait suddenly said, "What do you think of this Mum?" and dropped the shed skin onto my lap.

I was absolutely speechless and it took a full hour to get me off the ceiling, but once I could utter a few words, my knowledge of Anglo Saxon once again proved useful. Thank goodness Kait didn't have any pets nearby when she worked in the hair salon.

When Jordan, our eldest grandson. was a toddler, his father kept a selection of (to him) 'interesting' spiders, and being a responsible parent, he kept them in their tanks well away from the children, on 'sky hooks'.

One morning our daughter, Sophie, returned home with Jordan, after taking her daughter Robyn to school. She settled Jordan in the living room to play with his toys and went into the kitchen to sort out what was left of breakfast. She was busying away, when out of the corner of her eye she noticed a slight movement on the basket of washing. Eek! It was an escapee spider, the biggest of the collection, a hairy, brown tarantula.

How she kept quiet is a mystery, but not wanting to frighten either Jordan or the spider, she went into the hall, closed the door behind her and put all sorts of things along the bottom of the door so the spider had only the kitchen to explore, and then she summoned help. Had this spider and his friends known that morning that by tea time they would be sitting on a pet shop shelf awaiting new owners, they would have been rather surprised.

Robyn has inherited her father's interest for unusual pets and is the fond owner of a lovely snake, called 'Ginger'. Ginger's partner, Fred, died a while ago, so she lives alone in a large glass tank with wood chippings and small branches, and appears to sense when Robyn is about, coming up to the side of her tank for her tea – a dead mouse. Whatever happened to the little girl who could not bear to be parted from her fluffy red teddy?

FIREWORKS

Ted, and I would always try and watch the midnight fireworks, televised from London as one year ends and another begins.

The green firework painting, and the pink and blue, are of the display on the night when 2013 turned to 2014. Ted and I were sitting, glasses in hand (whiskey – not reading) as Big Ben rang out at midnight and the fireworks began. At the same time a loud thunderstorm broke overhead, here at Burley, with terrific lightning. The storm only ceased as the wonderful display ended.

Many years ago, my mother, who loved fireworks, died on Bonfire Night. Knowing her sense of humour, my brothers and I have wondered if she chose November 5th on purpose. Maybe the storm was her way of saying, "Hello."

FAREWELLS

This painting with the red fireworks, was inspired by the New Year's Eve display in 2013. It was bought by an elderly gentleman whose wife was seriously ill.

He wanted it as a reminder of a wonderful time he and his wife had spent in London before she was unwell.

Fireworks are wonderful to paint, with their startling colours … just the sort of palette for me. I gave Ted the fireworks treatment in the painting below. He was not always delighted to be my model and I caught him in a pensive mood – although in fact he was watching one of his favourite Cowboy films.

The photo below does him more justice and is just how I like to remember him.

When I started writing this book, Ted had not been well for some time and had become very frail, suffering from one chest infection to another. Sadly, he passed away, peacefully at home on February 2nd 2015, in his own bed, where he wanted to be.

Ironically, it would have been my Aunt Zona's 100th birthday. If she and my Uncle Jack had not taken The Coventry Arms at Corfe Mullen all those years ago, the chances are that Ted and I might never have met.

Ted's was a quiet end for a Good Man. I'm told by those who know, that the awful sadness will ease in time. I hope so.

His one great friend from his sea days died just three weeks before him, I like to think of them out there 'somewhere', reliving their glory days. When Ted and I meet again I shall be interested to hear what they've been up to.

THE FOOTBALL MATCH

I love get-togethers of any kind, and here I've painted a scene with which I expect most of you would be familiar – the match day. It could just as easily be the Sunday Grand Prix, or cricket, or tennis, although for the latter I expect there would be more women glued to the TV as well.

In the picture granny is enjoying the chance to do a bit of personal shopping … definitely not 'D.Ks'! The woman in the check dress is trying to interest her friends in a glass of wine, and her daughter is planning her son's birthday party, using the old, trusted, pass-me-down book on baking cakes.

Ted and I have been very lucky to have all our children and grandchildren living not too far away. Come rain or shine, coughs and colds, our family gathers together to celebrate ANYTHING.

Cake making is not exactly my forté, but when we get together for family birthdays it has become a tradition that I make a cake of sponge orientation. No two have ever been alike, although I always follow my Aunt Rene's recipe.

I recall one afternoon when I took the cake from the oven and I realised it was a complete disaster. Fortunately, I hadn't washed up the mixing bowl or hand whisk, so muttering to myself I put more ingredients into the bowl, and turning on the whisk too soon, found myself covered from head to waist in uncooked cake mixture from my first efforts.

My skills have since improved ... slightly.

THE VILLAGE SHOW

This painting is based on a village show from the days we were at The Swordsman, when Ted and I were running the beer tent. Our son Ben is the little boy with boxing gloves, taking part in the fancy dress competition.

We have an annual village show here in Burley in August, and people come from far and wide to join in – such is its reputation. My friends, Christine Coney and Brenda Farrell, and I have the Art Tent, where we exhibit our work and chat to people about the Burley Art Club exhibition and The Woodlanders exhibition, both of which start a few weeks later, although I must confess I spend a lot of the afternoon wandering about getting inspiration and just people watching.

THE PAGEANT

I have two paintings hanging in Burley Village Hall. One was commissioned by the hall committee in the year 2000, and it shows the flags, emblems, flowers and Royal regalia of Great Britain.

The first painting I did of this subject was much larger, five foot by just under two foot, and was the centre piece for a celebratory exhibition by Romsey Art Group, at Lee, near Romsey.

It was felt that there was nowhere in Burley Village Hall that the original would fit, so I was asked for a smaller version.

The second painting, shown on the opposite page, is the result of drawings, sketches, photos and memories, put together to depict the Burley Village celebrations for the Queen's Diamond Jubilee in 2012.

So much happened over the four days of celebration – flag raising, garden parties, a Youth of Burley (otherwise known as 'YOBs') party for the children and their families in the vicarage garden, games, and concerts in which so much local talent erupted on stage with singing, music and dancing. There was a school party with the children dressed in red, white and blue, during which each child was presented with a Diamond Jubilee mug by Burley's own Rt. Hon Desmond Swayne M.P.

AND there was a magnificent afternoon pageant, in which so many villagers took part that it was amazing there were enough people left in the crowd to cheer them on! The Pageant told the history of Burley through the ages, up to the present day. All walks of life were represented, including the church choir, the fire brigade, smugglers, ponies, servicemen of today and yesteryear, and much more.

At the end of the afternoon, tea and cakes were served by WI ladies dressed as Lyons Corner House 'Nippies', and we were treated to a display of maypole dancing by the school children, and a threatening Green Man.

The next day, we held our Sunday church service in the marquee on the green. Over that weekend we had picnics on the green, with plenty of food and wine … and fish and chips to boot!

Those four days were the best fun in all the years we have lived in Burley, thanks to the great organisers and the village as a whole. Hopefully, my painting reflects the feelings of that weekend. I have included all the happenings, but I deliberately didn't paint portraits of any of the people ... just suggestions. If anyone sees someone they recognise though, they could be right!

I put 'The Pageant' painting in the Burley Art Club's exhibition on the following August. It was bought for the village by the Parish Council and now hangs in the Village Hall, alongside the legend shown here on the left.

When I go off to the big studio in the sky, I hope people will continue to look at it and remember a great time.

THE OTHER PAGEANT

I have thought twice about writing about this other pageant, but my son, Ben, says I ought to. I think it is his way of getting his own back. He reminded me of the pageant that he took part in as a small boy of six.

The Medieval Pageant, according to the teachers, was to take place at Old Sarum, and all the local schools were to be involved, Dinton School no exception, with 'our' children playing the parts of villagers and artisans.

Ben came home from school to tell me, "Mum, I am going to be a spy, and I'm going to be executed."

Apparently I said, "Oh, that's lovely Ben, You will need a costume. I'll start straight away." And I did, looking through my 'History of Costume' books, and thoroughly enjoying making the outfit on his behalf.

Ben is a grown man now, with a son of his own, but he often tells me how appalled he was at my reaction on hearing of his planned execution.

He lay awake, unable to get to sleep, imagining his execution, for all the nights leading up to the event, but never said a word to anyone, not even to his Grandma, who lived opposite us.

It never occurred to us that he thought it was for real. We just thought he might have been a bit put out as we are unable to go and see him in the pageant, because we weren't able to get cover for the pub.

When the day arrived it was made even worse for him when another boy was taken away to the same 'fate' and didn't return. Ben waited for his turn, appalled to be wearing the costume that I had so happily made for what he thought was going to be his own 'execution'.

Poor Ben, I am amazed he ever spoke to us again.

CARNIVAL

I often think it strange that people say the British are reserved. Go to a pageant or a carnival in any village or town, or city, and you can see this is so far from the truth.

Some years ago, my greetings cards were printed by Dolphin Printers in Poole, and on one of my visits to them, the lady who chose the images they wanted, mentioned to me that she and a few dancing friends were going to put on a display of, as I thought she said, 'ballet dancing' at the forthcoming Ringwood Carnival Parade.

I thought this was not to be missed, so there I was, standing in the crowd with my two eldest grandchildren, Robyn and Jordan, both of whom were quite young at the time and were looking forward to seeing 'Granny's friend' ... and there she was, leading a troupe of 'belly dancers'!

It was a cold evening, but the energetic ladies certainly warmed up the thoughts of the red-blooded Ringwood males.

WAITING IN THE RAIN

I love it when people create little parades of their own … looking in shop windows, walking into church, queuing for tickets, or waiting for the bus, that's when you realise how different everybody is.

I've deliberately not put a setting to this painting, other than the fact that it is set in a rainstorm. I just wanted to concentrate on people, colour, pattern and umbrellas, but in all honesty I dislike umbrellas intensely, especially other people's, as at five foot two inches tall I am the wrong height and more than once have been poked in the eye by a taller person's 'brolly. Coats with hoods are much easier.

Even though the people in this painting are standing close together, they are keeping themselves to themselves. The only connection between them is the German Shepherd, who is showing a great interest in the old man's shopping bag … what could be in it – a juicy steak?

I originally called this painting 'Summertime in Ringwood', but it could be anywhere, especially on the January day that I sit and write this, as it been raining for days, high winds and floods throughout the country, and tens of thousands of people have endured a miserable, cold wet Christmas and New Year.

SHARED NAUGHTINESS

And now after all that rain, for bit of indulgence at the end of the book … These two paintings are based on a similar idea – that of two friends sharing something slightly naughty.

In the first painting the treat is a bag of delicious cakes, just bought from the bakery, and probably against the doctor's orders as both ladies are 'well-upholstered', … as also is the Pug dog who is hoping for a share of cake.

In the second painting, it's a risqué seaside postcard that the friends are looking at.

Our beach belles are off next to find a quiet corner and a couple of deckchairs, so they can observe all the goings on and people on the beach.

The card will be posted later, but who chose it? Was it the larger, bossy lady or the timid soul – and who is the guilty one sending it to?

May life be full of these moments!

So here we have it – memories of a farmer's daughter, a seafarer's wife, a pub landlady, a mother, an artist and a granny.

In my paintings I try to tell of a life full of fun, love and laughter, animals, friends and, most importantly, family. They have all been an inspiration with their funny ways and support. Without them all, including in-laws and out-laws, and especially my patient husband, Ted, my life and my paintings would never have been the same.